"Like a rollicking conversation with your best girlfriends—honest, intimate, and hilarious—Andy Steiner's down-to-earth guide to breastfeeding is a refreshing blend of straight talk and practical wisdom."

—**Karen Olson,** editor, *Utne* magazine

"If you're having a baby, do yourself a favor—ditch some of the mommy manuals and read this instead."

—**Monika Bauerlein,** senior editor, *Mother Jones*

"Andy Steiner is the woman to turn to for all the nursing issues that get glossed over. In the weirdly political world of breastfeeding, Steiner stands out as a sympathetic compadre. She knows the difficulties, the rewards, and the judgments that come with infant feeding."

—**Jennifer Niesslein and Stephanie Wilkinson,** editors, *Brain, Child: The Magazine for Thinking Mothers*

"In this spirited mamafesto, Andy Steiner boldly and wisely challenges myths not only about the process and protocol of breastfeeding itself, but about what our culture expects—often unfairly—of its mothers. Steiner and her fellow breastfeeders share their stories of both the joys and the, well, letdowns of lactation in voices that are so blunt, sassy, and loving you'll want to keep them around even after the breast pumps and nursing bras are packed away."

—**Andi Zeisler,** editor, *Bitch* magazine

"This is not your mother's how-to book about breastfeeding! Andy Steiner is a fresh voice: lively, informative, sassy, personal. The result is a book that will empower and comfort women who are breastfeeding, or thinking about it, and will even engage and inform those who aren't."

—**Mollie Hoben,** founding publisher, *Minnesota Women's Press*

"Andy Steiner's brave and honest book is a helpful companion during the tenuous process of learning to nurse, *and* learning to accept the social awkwardness about exposing our breasts that ironically pervades our culture. I smiled in recognition and was heartened by her attitude and suggestions."

—**Nanci Olesen,** producer and host, *MOMbo,* a radio resource for moms

"This is a wonderfully wide-ranging book. Women who love breastfeeding, those who find it incredibly difficult, strange, or painful; and those who don't yet know what they will decide or experience, will all feel welcome in *Spilled Milk*.... If you've ever breastfed, or thought you might, this is a book you'll want to read."

—**Faulkner Fox**, author, *Dispatches from a Not-So-Perfect Life*

"Instead of guilting moms with 'best for baby' moralizing, Steiner serves up a warm chat-fest of real-life mama experiences that help readers make fully-informed choices. And because of its big-picture look at breast-feeding's impact on sex, love, and life in general, this book provides an engaging preview of life during Babytime that any would-be mom will prize."

—**Helen Cordes**, editor, *Daughters* magazine

"I loved this book. It's humorous, honest, and empowering without being unrealistic. It paints a very full, complex, and real picture of what it's like to breastfeed—and that's exactly what moms need."

—**Nancy Gruver**, founder and publisher, *New Moon Magazine*

"*Spilled Milk* is filled with the voices of the wise and witty girlfriends I wish I had had when my first baby was born and I was struggling to keep the milk bar open 'round the clock. It's warm, compassionate, funny, and just the thing for a late-night nurse-a-thon."

—**Beth Hawkins**, senior editor, *City Pages* (Minneapolis)

"Wise, witty, deliciously reassuring. The perfect pick-me-up for mothers convinced that they're the only ones on the planet who are doing it wrong—which is pretty much all of us."

—**Barbara Graham**, author, *Women Who Run with the Poodles*

"A deliciously important book. Myth-busting and empowering, this is the real deal about nursing from real moms."

—**Ariel Gore**, editor, *Hip Mama*

Spilled Milk

Breastfeeding Adventures
and Advice from
Less-Than-Perfect Moms

Andy Steiner

RODALE

© 2005 by Andy Steiner

Book design by Christina Gaugler

Library of Congress Cataloging-in-Publication Data

Steiner, Andy.
    Spilled milk : breastfeeding adventures and advice from less-than-perfect
moms / Andy Steiner.
        p.   cm.
    Includes index.
    ISBN-13 978–1–59486–040–9 paperback
    ISBN-10 1–59486–040–8 paperback
    1. Breastfeeding—Popular works.   I. Title.
RJ216.S83   2005
649'.33—dc22   2005009989

Distributed to the trade by Holtzbrinck Publishers

2   4   6   8   10   9   7   5   3   1   paperback

To my mother

Contents

Acknowledgments

I still remember when I decided to write this book. It was in the middle of a dark, cold February night, and I was up nursing my oldest girl. I've always felt miserable being awake when the rest of the world is asleep, but over the years I've come to realize that those quiet hours with a warm baby can be the source of many a good idea.

The list of people who helped move this book from middle-of-the-night musing to the reality you now hold in your hands is long. First of all, I'd like to thank the scores of mothers who shared their breastfeeding stories with me. Many are named in the book, but there were countless others I didn't have space to include. Even if their names aren't mentioned, their stories and voices add flavor and authenticity. This book would not exist without them.

I also owe a debt of gratitude to the many people who told others about this project, including Dorie Lanni, Sharis Ingram, Deborah Martin, Wendy Manning, Sasha Aslanian, Laura Coleman, Karin Bultman, Christina Hayward, Lisa Jervis, Anne La Fave, Rachel McGarry, Mary Johnson, Monika Bauerlein, Betsy Lawson, Maja Beckstrom, Amy Nelson, Berry Steiner, Laine Bergeson, Betsy Carpenter, Kara Lubin, Becky Sun, Miriam Karmel, and Julie Lund. The fact that I was able to speak with so many amazing mamas is testament to the power of women's friendships as much as it is to the Internet. My original e-mail request for interviews was passed from friend to friend around the United States and the world. The response was overwhelming—and heartening.

Two key people helped make this book a reality, including my wondrous agent, Catherine Fowler, of the Redwood Agency, who sought me out and—best of all—believed in my potential. I also could not have asked for a better editor than the mighty Mariska van Aalst, who *got it*—every single word.

Thanks to Hugh Delehanty for his expert counsel and kind recommendation, Cathy Madison for her sharp proofreader's eye and friendly support, Chris Dodge for his flawless early research expertise, and Hilary Bullock for her ability to turn a sow's ear into a silk purse. Kudos go to Nancy Austin, Carolyn Chisholm, and Sarah Eastwold for keeping my children happy and occupied while I slaved away at my keyboard. Then there's my midwife, Edie Ziegler, and the lactation staff at Regions Hospital in St. Paul, Minnesota, who helped both of my girls have the beautiful early babyhoods they deserved.

Last but not least, to my love and best friend, John: Thank you for your unending patience, measured advice, and good humor. And to Astrid and Iris: Thank you for serving as unknowing inspiration and gentle reminders of the passage of time.

Introduction

Why I Needed This Book— And Why You Do, Too

Five years ago, I was a breastfeeding expert. I'd read all the books, I'd taken a class, and I'd even observed other mothers in action. I was a pro.

Then my daughter was born.

It didn't take long (something like two minutes) for me to realize that I—or my *breasts,* to be more specific—were now responsible for feeding the squirmy, frightened-looking thing that my husband had just placed on my chest. This, I remembered from the books I'd studied, was the moment when my baby was supposed to be gently guided to the breast, where she would instinctively latch on. Suddenly, magically, we'd be transformed into an efficient, loving nursing team.

But my life—and most likely yours—doesn't often resemble the soft-focus, laid-back lives that get written about in the nursing manuals. I should've known better than to think that I would carry breastfeeding off with earth-motherly aplomb, but I figured that I'd worried enough about everything else that had to do with having a baby. It couldn't be all that hard to breastfeed, right?

Wrong. For me, at least, learning how to breastfeed *was* hard. I'm not talking *impossibly* hard, like tearing-my-hair-out hard, but more like icing-on-the-freaky-cake-that-is-first-time-motherhood hard. Overwhelmingly hard. Stressfully hard. Even painfully hard. But also *beautifully* hard. When my daughter and I finally got our nursing routine down pat (and even before we had it all figured out), there were moments at the breast so sweet and wonderful that I thought my heart would burst with love. But there were also moments when I felt confused, frightened, sad, and—worst of all—alone.

From the outside, at least, it seemed to me that every other mother-baby team I saw nursed more or less gracefully, like Madonna and child. Not me and my kid. In the beginning, we looked more like Laurel and Hardy. Still, I was determined to do the best that I could for her. So I bumbled through breast-pump explosions, indecent exposures, late-night crying fits (both hers *and* mine), and not one but three raging cases of the dreaded breast infection, mastitis. Later on, I found out that almost all breastfeeding mothers could tell horror stories that rivaled mine, that even the most graceful Madonnas or defiant tit-slinging lactivists had moments of fear, doubt, or just plain embarrassment—times when they felt like throwing in the towel, or at least fading into the furniture.

This is the truth, but I figured it out later, after the fact. When I was in the thick of things, when an adorable eight-pound stranger had turned my nights into days and my brain into mush, I didn't think to turn to any of the mamas I knew for support. Instead, I tried going through the pile of breastfeeding books I'd amassed pre-baby, hoping to find some reassurance that I wasn't alone. Although the books provided reams of practical charts and illustrations about the mechanics of breastfeeding, what was missing, I quickly realized, were real-life stories and informed advice from women who'd *been there*—funky, opinionated broads whose humorous, sensitive, and even ribald tales would've taken a load off my sagging new-mom shoulders.

I wanted a book that read like a 2:00 A.M. support group, a book that said, in a warm, understanding voice: "Don't worry about it, honey. It's tough at first, but it'll get better. And if it doesn't, it's not the end of the world." I wanted a book that would help me laugh when I felt like crying.

Because I am a journalist, I often seek my answers through the experiences of others. So when I decided to write this book, I set out to interview women around the country about their breastfeeding experiences, to ask them to bare all in candid conversations about this formative—but rarely discussed—experience. In the course of each interview, I asked subjects to provide tips for nursing mothers—indispensable advice they wish someone would've given them when times (or titties) got tough. The result is a rollicking discussion about what can only be called the world's first fast food.

Bosom Buddies

Lord knows women like to talk. I've been in book groups and knitting groups, on lunch dates and at nights on the town where the chatter flows fierce and free, where everything is discussed and nothing is off-limits. But before my friends and I started having children of our own, the topic of breastfeeding rarely came up.

In America, we tend to avoid talking about the *functional* uses of our breasts. So nursing's not something that gets discussed casually, like, "Nice shirt. How's that engorgement problem going?" But as soon as this book gave me an excuse to broach the subject with almost any woman I met, it was like pulling the little Dutch boy's finger out of the dike. The stories just came flooding out.

What do current and former nursing mothers want to talk about? The topics are myriad, from start-up struggles and pumping protocol to weaning worries. This book compiles those stories in chapters designed to guide first-time (and second- or third- or fourth-time) mothers through the haze of breastfeeding, from a baby's very first moments in the world to the day a mother packs up her pump for good. The accounts are reassuring, uncensored, and—best of all—sometimes pretty funny. But mostly, they're just *real*.

"At first, it didn't feel easy or even natural at all," laughs Deb, a New Hampshire nurse-practitioner and mother of one. "Even though I knew better, deep inside I always expected that you'd stick the baby on your boob and she'd start sucking and everything would be cake from there. I didn't expect my nipples to be sore and hurt or—

because my daughter was born in the middle of the summer—to dread daytime feedings because she felt so hot and sticky." Maybe it's because Deb's daughter is now in third grade, but something about the topic makes her cackle almost wickedly: "It turns out that breastfeeding was exactly like everything else about having a kid. Nothing goes the way you expect it to. So it's better not to expect anything."

(Gentle reader: I hope that hearing about other mothers' struggles won't discourage you from taking on the breastfeeding challenge. I'm willing to gamble that you can handle the truth. Knowing that you're not alone will help give you the strength that you need to keep going.)

Most women do have expectations about what it takes to be a good mother. And most of us also think—deep down inside—that we know the right way to care for children. If you're committed to breastfeeding in a world where conveniently packaged formula is available in every corner store, clearly you must think that nursing is worth the effort. But once your baby is born and you have a moment to take a deep breath and look around, you'll quickly realize that one woman's *effort* could easily be another woman's deal breaker. No one in the world raises their kids exactly the way you raise yours. This means that you don't have all the answers and that you shouldn't try to provide them for anybody else. Because smart women can't survive without their girlfriends, maybe your new-mama mantra could become: *Withhold judgment. Learn from experience.*

Mary, a forty-year-old mother of three from St. Paul, Minnesota, has always been one of those women who make breastfeeding—not to mention pregnancy and labor—seem like a walk in the park. After a relatively smooth introduction, she nursed her oldest son until just before his first birthday and her second for nine months. When her third boy was born, Mary just assumed that nursing *him* would be as easy as nursing his brothers. But it wasn't. At all.

Mary and her new baby were home from the hospital for just two days when her nipples began to crack and bleed. "I'll never forget the way I felt," she says. "I was just sitting on the couch, crying. I've got this red, swollen breast. It's the middle of the summer, all the shades are drawn, and my nipples are bleeding all over the place. It was a real low point."

Particularly discouraging for Mary was the fact that here she was, a seasoned pro at the mama game, and for some reason she still couldn't seem to get her new baby comfortably settled and nursing. While professionals bend over backward to help a first-time mother work through her breastfeeding problems, Mary discovered that a third-timer often gets pushed to the end of the line. "You should be able to figure this out for yourself," the nurses, doctors, and lactation consultants seemed to be saying. "If you can't, then maybe you just aren't trying hard enough."

Because she had two other young children to care for, Mary felt like she was being torn in every possible direction. She wanted to get her new baby latched, but she also needed to change her two-year-old's diaper and help her four-year-old learn how to ride his new bike. Guiltily, she realized that she just didn't have enough time to get this newest member of her brood nursing efficiently.

"I called my sister," Mary recalls. "She's a midwife. She said to me, 'If it hurts so bad, you should just stop.'" Her sister's blessing was all the permission Mary needed to give up on breastfeeding. She went to the store and bought bottles and formula that very day.

Over the years, Mary has had flashes of guilt about her hastily made decision—especially when other mothers seemed to judge her for bottlefeeding her baby—but despite everything, her youngest son continues to thrive.

"He might be a little skinnier than the others," Mary says, "but he's a fabulous child. He hasn't had the health problems that his brothers had. He hardly ever had an ear infection, and the other ones both had to have tubes put in. He tested into the gifted program at school. He survived—and so did I."

For Mary, the hardest part about the experience was the feeling of failure and her perception that other mothers thought of her as a "lazy bottlefeeder." There were days early on when she wanted to wear a sign around her neck that said, "Bleeding nipples! Extreme pain! Two other children!"—anything to explain why she had chosen to feed her precious baby formula rather than mother's milk.

The impulse to kick each other when we're down can be a hard habit to break. I'm hoping that this book will encourage well-meaning women to hop off the judgment train and really try to understand why mothers do the things they do. From now on, I'm firmly in the corner of any mama who's out to do the best she can for her kiddies. I hope others will do the same for me.

"I think women can be hard on each other and on themselves," observes Laura, a daily-newspaper columnist and mother of two. "Breastfeeding seems to be one of those hot topics. Everybody has an opinion about it, and most of us can be quick to judge. It ends up being motherhood in a microcosm."

What This Book Is. What This Book Is Not.

To be a mother is to feel guilty. No matter what sacrifices you make for your child, there is always another mother who's given up more, achieved more, made it look easier. But guilt isn't the only negative emotion that motherhood inspires. To be a mother is also to feel defensive.

Take Michelle, a thirty-six-year-old health-care sales executive and mother of two from Plymouth, Minnesota. When she had breast-reduction surgery at age twenty-two, her surgeon warned her that the procedure could limit her future ability to breastfeed. She hardly gave it a second thought. Later, when she couldn't produce enough breast milk to feed her oldest son without formula supplements, Michelle felt guilty, but she also felt angry at anyone who assumed she was bottlefeeding her baby out of "greed or laziness."

"I made the decision that was right for me at the time," Michelle says defiantly. "And even after what I went through trying to breast-feed my kids, I still don't regret my choice. I have a friend who says her breasts are all gone after breastfeeding, but for some reason my boobs post-breastfeeding are still in pretty good shape. There's still a bit of lift left. I have to believe that if I hadn't had the surgery way back then, they'd be close to my belly button by now."

Anne, a thirty-six-year-old medical researcher, really wanted to breastfeed her son. But she also knew that there was a possibility that the medications she took to control her bipolar disorder could be passed through her breast milk. Determined to give her baby the best possible start in life, Anne stopped all of her medications until, during the fifth month of her pregnancy, she started to feel the familiar cloud of depression descending. By the time her son was born, Anne had started taking all of her medications again. "When I went back on lithium," she sighs, "I knew I wasn't going to breastfeed."

Later, when Anne and her infant son joined a mothers' group, she felt out of place when she realized that she was the only formulafeeder in the bunch. She felt alienated, guilty, and defensive, certain that the other mothers assumed she must be bottlefeeding out of vanity rather than necessity, yet she was reluctant to reveal her entire health history.

"There was always an assumption that I was going to breastfeed," Anne says, shaking her head, "and every time I pulled out the bottle, I always felt like I had to explain myself. What struck me as repellent was that the other mothers just assumed that breastfeeding was a possibility for everyone. All the time, I'd be thinking, 'You have the *privilege* to breastfeed, and I don't.' People assume that everyone can nurse their babies. But not everyone can. I don't want to be judged for that."

Laura breastfed her oldest son until he was a toddler. "There were a lot of mothers in the office who'd say, 'I can't believe you're still doing that,'" she recalls. "I felt almost embarrassed that I was still doing it, and I'd say sheepishly, 'Yeah, I'm just not ready to stop yet,' but inside I'd be saying, '*Of course* I'm still doing that. Only a selfish mother would give up so quickly.'" Laura thinks for a minute before adding, "Then again, who am I to judge other women's decisions? What makes me think that what's right for me is right for everybody else?"

Tina, a forty-year-old development director from Minneapolis, spent months trying to teach her preemie daughter to latch on to the breast. She observed other mothers hovering around their tiny babies in the intensive-care nursery, watching their awkward attempts at breastfeeding infants they could hold for only short periods at a time.

"I think I wanted to breastfeed my daughter because my mom had breastfed me and my sister back in the sixties, when hardly anyone else was doing it," Tina says. "I don't recall how my parents introduced us to the fact that we were breastfed, but there was a great deal of pride associated with it. Also, because my baby was a preemie, part of me wanted to be able to nurture her as much as possible because we hadn't been together for the entire pregnancy. And everyone in the hospital told me how important breast milk would be to her development."

Premature babies—Tina's daughter was born at just twenty-six weeks—often have a hard time developing a sucking impulse. Tina, a hardworking achiever who admits "when I want something to work, I tend to get a little fixated on it," watched as one by one, most of the other neonatal intensive-care unit (NICU) mothers switched to formula. She decided to stick it out—but only on her own terms.

"I was truly in the wilderness on this one," Tina recalls. "During the whole time that my daughter was in the hospital, I was extremely sensitive to judgment. I wanted to do the right thing for her, but I also didn't want anyone to tell me that I was being a bad mother if I couldn't provide a 'normal' experience for my child. For that reason, I guess, I was intimidated by breastfeeding support groups. Even though I really wanted to breastfeed, I needed it to also be okay for us not to succeed or to make the decision to use formula. I was afraid that the women at La Leche League would be so gonzo about breastfeeding that it would start to feel impossible for me to succeed. And besides, when my baby was so little and so sick, I didn't want to be around all of those happy, contented breastfeeding moms." Eventually—and much to Tina's delight—her daughter learned to latch like an old pro.

This book is pro-breastfeeding, to be sure, but it is not about making mothers who choose not to—or cannot—nurse, feel guilty. It's also not about making a mother like Kathy, a forty-year-old Olympia, Washington, devotee of attachment parenting, feel like a freak for continuing to breastfeed her four-year-old—with no wean date in site. "It's my choice," Kathy says. "It's what works for us."

My thoughts exactly. What worked for Anne and her son wasn't what worked for Kathy and her daughter. And what works for you and your kid may be something else altogether. What virtually all mamas have in common, I've discovered, is that we want the best for our children. How we define *best* is up to us.

Milk Tick

There's a picture of my kid that always cracks me up. It was taken when she was two or three months old. My little baby girl, who came out of the womb wrinkled and wizened like an old man, had miraculously transformed into a moon-faced cherub, a plumped-up nursing machine, a baby in a fat suit.

"When my girl got like that, we called her the Milk Tick," Deb says. "She was so fat and happy that she looked like she would burst. I remember I'd look at her and think, 'I did that.' It made me feel proud."

I felt proud, too. This kid, this exhausting, exasperating, awe-inspiring miracle, was *mine.* I made her, and now my milk was making her fat. I felt powerful.

Speaking of miracles, when I interviewed Tina, she brought along her daughter. I'd heard about this baby, even seen photos of a tiny infant no bigger than a man's hand, a weak little creature stuck with tubes and needles, swaddled in a clear-plastic NICU isolette. The baby I met at the coffee shop with Tina bore no resemblance to the one in those photos. She was round as a ball, alert, chubby even. I held her while Tina and I talked, and I watched her mother's eyes glow with the kind of naked, intimate pride that most people reserve only for their children.

"I can truly say I feel responsible for this," Tina says, gesturing toward her daughter. "She went from being the very tiniest one-pound mouse born way too soon to this healthy, robust twelve-pound baby. I don't say this about very many things, but I am so proud of her and what I've been able to do for her."

Though my kid isn't the only accomplishment in my life, she is the biggest. On good days, I still feel a kind of runner's high, like I've just crossed the finish line at a marathon. On bad days—and you'll read about plenty of them in this book—I wish I could just step aside and let someone else do the running for me.

It's important to realize that motherhood is nothing like a race. For one thing, there's no finish line. And, like it or not, there's no turning back and retreating into the crowd. From here on out, no matter what happens, you'll always be a mother. Hopefully, reading this book and learning from the experiences of other women will help make the road a little bit smoother, and when the starting gun goes off, you'll leap out of the blocks, ready for anything.

Spilled Milk

Chapter I

Far from the Land of Milk and Honey

Breastfeeding SEEMS like it should be easy, but it's not—at first

Poor Rachel. A little over four months pregnant with her first child and still just contemplating breastfeeding, the thirty-year-old PhD student is being treated to an earful of horror stories by a rowdy group of lactation veterans, women who'd *been there* and *done that,* who'd nursed their children for an average of a year apiece and are excited to chat about the experience—warts and all.

The group had gathered to talk about breastfeeding, but the talk—as estrogen-fueled conversations tend to do—quickly wanders into other territories, like motherhood, work, relationships, body image, and sex. Fueled on brownies, fruit, and caffeine, these six women, educated professionals in their thirties, are in the mood to dish the dirt. When the topic turns to establishing a breastfeeding relationship in the first few days and weeks of a baby's life, the stories practically leap out of their mouths.

"I had a really hard time when my oldest was starting nursing," Maja, a thirty-five-year-old newspaper reporter, says. "He was really colicky, and every time I'd try to nurse him, he'd back off and scream bloody murder. I remember being a couple of weeks into all of this and having dinner with my husband and mother and step-father, when I burst into tears. I just started sobbing. I blurted out," Maja fakes a tear-strained voice: "'This is so much worse than childbirth!'"

I know the feeling. During the raw, early days of first-time mother-hood, I often felt like a ticking time *boob*. Anything could set me off, and more often than not, the things that got me really worked into a froth had to do with breastfeeding. It was just so much more com-plicated than anyone told me it would be. I felt awkward, anxious, frustrated, and *responsible*—about as far from a "natural mother" as a gal could be.

Maja's story gets everyone laughing—a few even nod know-ingly—and so she continues, encouraged:

"My labor was *long*. I mean, I pushed for four hours. But it was over once he was born, and now nothing had prepared me for this second tough period. Here I was two weeks into nursing, and I was still feeling so inadequate. I had assumed that this was something that would be natural. It would just click, but it didn't. It was really painful, and I couldn't imagine getting through it."

A couple of the women cast concerned glances in expectant-mama Rachel's direction. Among many current or former nursing mothers, there's an impulse to gloss over the tougher parts of breast-feeding, an unspoken worry that if you tell a mother-to-be anything but happy, blissful stories about babes at the breast, they'll bail for the "convenience" of formula. Still, for these women, the desire to tell their own stories wins out.

"Somehow it gradually got better. At some point, I realized, 'I enjoy this.' But there was no enjoyment in that early stage. I re-member thinking it was at least a couple of months before I actu-ally enjoyed nursing at all." In the end, Maja nursed her son for seventeen months.

Back when I was pregnant, my husband and I had joined a group of other expectant parents at our hospital's breastfeeding class. The two-hour meeting was the crashest of crash courses, I realize now, but at the time (about fifty minutes or so in) I remember thinking,

"It's basically just baby to boob. What else can be *said* about this topic?" We cradled baby dolls, listened to the lactation consultant's pep talk, and passed around flash cards detailing the benefits of breast milk. All good news. All very predictable. So when this klatch of loose-talking breastfeeders launches in on the not-so-rosy realities, I feel that five years ago, talk like this might've sent me running for the hills. I want to figure out how to strike that balance between telling the whole truth and encouraging newbie moms, like Rachel, to give it a shot.

"Both of my kids had breast-milk jaundice when they were newborns," brags Elizabeth, a freelance writer. "The doctor told me they had jaundice from my breast milk. Imagine how that made me feel. My kids were orange until they were three months old."

"My issues have been more along the lines of body image," interjects Karin, a thirty-five-year-old health-care consultant. "I'm so tired of my big boobs. I don't like the way they look. Also, my son won't take a bottle, so too much of the time it's all up to me. I've had these moments where I really want a break. Sometimes I want to be gone for a whole day, but instead I'm stuck with my son."

"I thought, 'If I have to sleep in my bra for a year, I'm going to lose it,'" laughs Sasha, a thirty-five-year-old radio producer. "I didn't realize that it all regulates itself by six months. At the beginning, I planned every outfit based around"—here her voice turns ominous—The *"Leak Factor."*

Oh yes, we all know about the Leak Factor. Siri, a thirty-six-year-old curator, shares a Leak Factor story that sounds a little like an urban myth. "I had this friend who ran out to get some take-out food when her baby was really young," she says. "She produced *a lot* of milk, and she had soaked through a pad, a bra, a T-shirt, and a pair of bib overalls by the time she got there. She had so much milk that while she was nursing, she had to use a bottle to collect milk from the other side. She could collect something like four ounces that way."

Kristin, a thirty-two-year-old account manager, rolls her eyes. Clearly she can top that story: "At the beginning, pretty much all of the time I was soaking wet. I would soak through all of these nursing pads, and then I'd throw them in the garbage." She pauses for dramatic effect. "Well, we have a dachshund. They're scent hounds." Seeing where this is going, everyone cracks up. "She'd go and she'd dig through my garbage can, and later on I'd find wads of chewed-up nursing pads all over the house. Eventually she got a bowel obstruction from eating them."

As the laughter dies down, Rachel speaks up tentatively. "I really do admire the decision to nurse," she says, looking around the room, "but I just can't imagine, given how hard it's been for you to do everything . . ." Her voice trails off, and then she finally asks: "What makes you want to nurse for that long? Or even start in the first place?"

That's the million-dollar question, isn't it? But ask any breast-feeder, and you'll hear a million very good reasons.

Everyone in the room jumps to breastfeeding's defense.

"Once you get nursing down, it's so much easier than a bottle," Elizabeth says.

"You are providing the best possible nutrition for the baby," adds Siri. "Breast milk cures all ills. It is instantly calming. It helps the baby sleep."

Kristin gets a dreamy look in her eyes. "Then there are times like when your child is nursing and they're just wrapping up and they're kinda drowsy," she says. "My son would throw his arms back like this"—she puts her arms over her head—"and he'd have milk dribbling out of his mouth and a big smile on his face. I've never seen such a look of contentment."

"My son's start was so hard," Maja adds, "but it ended up being this wonderful experience. There are these times when my second son is hungry and he'll just open up his little mouth and go 'uh, uh, uh,' and you get this confident feeling like," she narrows her eyes and switchs to a sultry voice: "'I can fulfill your every desire.'"

Karin smiles. "Sometimes he'll be nursing and he gets tired and his little hand starts moving all over my face."

"I had a hair puller," Kristin adds almost wistfully.

Then Maja gives us all something to think about. "I have a friend who doesn't have any children, and one day I was complaining about how much time nursing took up. She said, 'You know, it's going to be over so fast.' I remember thinking that even though she didn't have the experience herself, she was just so wise. Now, when I'm nursing my baby to sleep and I find myself thinking, 'I've got to go make one more call for work,' I remember my friend's words, and I'll just settle into enjoying that incredibly intimate moment. I wouldn't have missed that opportunity for the world."

Welcome to the Sorority

To bring a new baby into the world is to say goodbye to life as you know it. For a few days, weeks, or months, formerly quiet, adult-friendly households experience an acutely disturbing loss of control; an already chaotic family can simply be turned on its head. It's a painful, lengthy hazing ritual—a rite of passage—where a woman enters as an innocent and comes out a *mother*—bruised and battered, perhaps, but ultimately one of the strongest creatures on the planet.

At first, babies seem to need everything, and the adults entrusted with their care and feeding often find themselves at a loss to understand how to make and keep these vulnerable little creatures happy. Because parents (face it) are the source of *everything*—food, comfort, life itself—for their newborn children, breastfeeding mothers often feel overwhelmed by this awesome responsibility. When nursing isn't a textbook-smooth experience from birth—and more often than not it isn't—many mothers quickly become discouraged.

When a new mom doesn't have the support she needs to get through the rough spots, the temptation to throw in the towel and pick up the formula can be pretty strong. And, honestly, who can blame a mother with a squalling infant and an aching breast for giving in and giving a bottle? Even though studies reporting the benefits of breast milk have been widely related in the media, formula is still readily available, widely advertised, and in the beginning at least, comparatively neat and tidy. Plus, if you're like most American women of childbearing age, you've probably grown up with few examples of openly breastfeeding mothers, so you might not have many women to turn to when problems arise. This means that if you're going to succeed at breastfeeding, you've got to be pretty determined.

"For the most part, our moms did not breastfeed us, and our friends are delaying childbirth or they are not breastfeeding. So there's not a community of breastfeeders out there like there used to be [before our mother's time]," explains Deborah Dee, MPH, who is doing research at the University of North Carolina-Chapel Hill School of Public Health on the impact that breastfeeding-support programs can have on low-income women in rural North Carolina. Dee believes that the relatively low rates of breastfeeding in her region, and in the country as a whole, are due to a number of deeply embedded societal factors, including a low level of community support for nursing mothers and the general acceptance of formula-feeding as a viable, healthy option for infants.

"Part of the problem is that we are in this transitional period of more women going back to breastfeeding, but we don't have that seasoned knowledge base anymore," she explains. "In the distant past, if there were latch problems, for instance, a woman could talk to her mother or sister or her neighbor, and that person would say, 'Oh, you have to do this. Let me show you.' Now it has become so much more official and time-intensive. You have to call a lactation consultant or go to a La Leche League meeting. And if you are back to work already or you have other small children, how do you find the time to do that? There's been a breakdown in support for breastfeeding, and that's what's making it harder for women these days."

Catherine Adeboye, RN, IBCLC, a lactation consultant at Regions Hospital in St. Paul, Minnesota, says that women who somehow come to believe that nursing in all cases is an easy, natural act are more likely to give up when times get tough.

"Sometimes moms feel like they've been sold a bill of goods," she says. "The books and the literature they give out at the clinic say,

'Try breastfeeding. It's easy. It's natural. It's convenient.' But for most women, the first month is not easy or natural or convenient. It's a lot of work and maybe even some struggle. Women need to know that ahead of time. But they also need to know that eventually most mothers get to the point where breastfeeding *is* easy, natural, and convenient. Most moms love nursing their babies once they get past those early struggles."

Call it The Hump, The Lump, The Awkward Stage. Or call it something much worse. (Sometimes, I still remember the first few weeks of my daughter's life by the endearing name I'd given them: The Shits.) While the first few hours of a baby's life are essential to getting a child started on the breast, it's the days and weeks *after* mother and child leave the hospital that are often what ultimately determine the success of the nursing relationship. Babies who seemed to latch on correctly at the hospital mysteriously begin losing weight. Mothers with constant nursers start to feel like worn-down, broken-down milking machines. Babies fuss and cry for hours on end, the breast providing only fleeting relief. It's a depressing thought, I know, and if this is your first time through it, it may seem like it will never end.

But it will, and it does, even when you feel like Robin from Ontario, Canada, who added this post to the mothering.com bulletin board: "Where are all the pleasurable feelings I'm supposed to be getting from nursing? Where are the relaxing hormones? . . . I feel like I'm losing my mind."

Jane Swigart, PhD, a San Francisco psychotherapist and author of *The Myth of the Perfect Mother: Parenting without Guilt*, believes that the postpartum period can be one of the most trying times of a woman's life—both emotionally and physically. Mothers are adjusting to a new life, a new family, and a new set of responsibilities. Learning to breastfeed at the same time as an infant—babies aren't born knowing how it works—adds to the stress for new mothers.

"Having a new baby is lonely and terrifying, mainly because you are in an altered state and so extremely vulnerable," Dr. Swigart says. "For a time, you revert back to when you were a little baby.

That's normal, but for some women it's terrifying. I remember when I was trying to breastfeed my daughter when she was a newborn, and my sister looked at me and said, 'You're going to smother the baby!' It totally unnerved me. People say the most horrible, ignorant things during that time, and if you don't know better, you have no backbone to stand up to that."

That sense of vulnerability may be at the heart of why so many mothers quit breastfeeding at the first sign of trouble. We mothers are tough, gutsy creatures—no one can call giving birth a wimpy act, for instance—but there are plenty of times early on when a mama needs to be reminded of her strength.

"It's very easy to undermine a mother's confidence during the time right after a birth," Adeboye says. "And once that confidence in the ability to breastfeed is undermined, I don't think it ever comes back for some people. We try to remind mothers that they can do it, because the majority of the time, they can."

Fight for Your Right to Breastfeed

When Ola, a thirty-two-year-old artist from New York City's Washington Heights neighborhood, describes herself as "stubborn," there's a hint of pride in her voice. If she weren't so stubborn, she says, she would've given up on breastfeeding early on.

Ola's family were *not* breastfeeders. In fact, until she met her partner, and he explained that his mother breastfed him, she had barely even realized that babies could be fed from their mothers' breasts.

"I know it sounds crazy, but I didn't know anything about breastfeeding at all until I was pregnant," Ola says. "I didn't know people who did it. I honestly didn't know that you could feed your child without using milk or formula because I'd never seen it. It never happened in my family."

During her pregnancy, Ola read everything she could find about childrearing. While the experts had different perspectives on temper tantrums, teething, and the terrible twos, they all agreed on one thing: Breast milk is the best food for infants. The idea that her body could provide all the food her baby needed in the first months of life was a revelation for Ola. The idea of giving the milk from her breasts to her child made her feel powerful, like she possessed a hidden talent that she'd never even realized.

"As I got more and more pregnant and my breasts started filling up with the milk, I thought, 'This is great!'" Ola recalls. "Once I realized that this was something I could do, something that I was meant to do even, there was absolutely no turning back."

For a long time, Ola didn't even talk to her parents about her decision to breastfeed. She knew what their reaction would be. "My mom was going to freak out," Ola explains. "I didn't want to deal with that until I had to." So instead, she turned to her partner's mother, asking the older woman for advice and guidance. After Ola's daughter was born—by emergency Cesarean—her mother-in-law moved in for a few days to assist with the new baby and with establishing breastfeeding.

"I don't know what I would've done without her," Ola says. "She's a real breastfeeding advocate. She's very supportive, and she helped me get over the early humps."

The humps Ola faced at the start were far from insurmountable. Despite a few classic latch-on problems, the first days of breastfeeding were nearly textbook-perfect. Having an experienced guide on hand helped. "The only problem I ran into at the beginning was latching on," she recalls. "That was the hardest part. I needed to make sure that she got everything in her mouth." (When she says *everything*, Ola means that her baby needed to learn to latch on not just to the nipple but also to the areola—the area surrounding the nipple.) "I needed to perfect my hold, too, but once I got past that point, it was smooth sailing. And once I figured out how I could lay down while feeding her," she drawls, laughing, "it was *ooo-ver.* I was chillin'."

After the baby was born, Ola had no way of hiding the fact that she was breastfeeding. Her mother and father were aghast.

"It was a huge problem for them," Ola says. "They'd say stuff like, 'She's not going to grow. She's not going to be strong. She's not going to be healthy. You need to give her formula. That's how you can monitor what she's getting.' Of course, I was a new mother and very nervous about my daughter's health, so hearing them say stuff like that made me anxious."

Still, at that moment, some sense of inner resolve kicked in for Ola. Even though she was feeling weak and vulnerable from the surgery, she told her parents to back off, insisting that she knew what was best for her child.

"I was pretty determined," Ola admits. "The more my parents resisted it, the more I wanted to do it. I wanted to prove them wrong. She was growing so nicely. She was so healthy and strong. I felt like I was doing the right thing. I guess at that time I was just following my "mother's intuition," letting my true nature take over. I was adamant that nobody was going to tell me what to do with my baby."

Eventually, Ola and her parents worked out an awkward sort of truce, with Ola continuing to breastfeed openly and her mother continuing to push formula in her own less-than-subtle way.

"She bought cases of formula," Ola laughs. "She'd bring them over to my house. It was just horrible, but it was also funny. They never got over it."

Breastfeeding has worked so well that Ola plans to let her now-toddler-aged daughter nurse until she weans herself. Ola describes her mothering style as "intuitive" parenting. "I haven't made any real conscious decisions around rules or education or discipline," she explains. "I kind of flow as I go. So breastfeeding works for us, because it's easy and natural, and that's what I'm all about."

And though she wishes her mother and father would have kept their opinions about nursing to themselves, Ola says she doesn't blame them for their insistence that formula is better for infants than breast milk. In her neighborhood, she says, that's the prevailing belief. "Even at the hospital when my daughter was born, the nurses were handing me the formula, saying stuff like, 'Take this for when you get tired,'" Ola recalls. "I'd say. 'No. I'm going to breastfeed her,' and then they said, 'You are going to get tired.' I was like, 'How can you say I'm going to get *tired* of feeding my daughter?'"

Despite her mother's relentless efforts to get her to stop, Ola has no regrets about her decision to breastfeed. In fact, she says, it's one of the best things she's done since she became a mother.

"When I thought about using formula, I was concerned about allergies, and what kind would be the best to buy, and how I would mix it all up and keep the bottles clean and sterilized," she says. "In the end, it seemed like a lot more work and worry than just lifting up my shirt."

Double the Fun

For many mothers, nursing eventually becomes as easy as lifting up a shirt, but when you have a hungry set of twins to feed, it can be a completely different story. Take it from Jackie, a twenty-five-year-old community college instructor from Baltimore, Maryland.

When she learned she was pregnant, Jackie planned on breast-feeding, but when she found out that she was carrying twins, she quickly adopted what she calls a "realistic and reasonable" attitude about the daunting task that lay ahead. Her husband pledged his support for whatever decision she made, and Jackie agreed to give nursing a try in the hospital—but with the caveat that she could give up at any time if the responsibility grew to be more than she could handle.

"I really wanted to breastfeed, because I thought it was the best thing for my babies," Jackie says, "but almost from the beginning, I didn't think I was going to be able to do it for as long as other people did. It just seemed like it would be way too much work, and I wasn't sure if I had the backbone required to really follow through with it."

Then Jackie gave birth to her daughters—one vaginally, the second with the help of a Cesarean. The experience left Jackie feeling like she had been run over by a truck. Painkillers helped ease the discomfort of the Cesarean incision, but they also left her feeling weak and woozy.

One of Jackie's daughters had jaundice, and this made her sleepy and less interested in nursing. She had to be woken up before each feeding. Jackie's other daughter had a poor latch, and had to be repositioned several times during each meal.

Jackie had originally planned on feeding both of her daughters at the same time. This technique, called tandem nursing, can be difficult to master, but once a mother's gets it down, it can cut feeding times in half. Jackie worked on her tandem nursing skills at the hospital, and with the help of what felt like an army of nurses and a platoon of pillows, she was able to get both babies latched on at once. Because of the Cesarean, she wasn't able to lift or turn comfortably, so Jackie needed extra assistance to get the babies positioned.

In the relative comfort of the hospital, Jackie slowly began to gain confidence in her ability to successfully nurse two babies. "I had this big, huge bed that was adjustable and all these pillows around me and experts there who could help me, so I never felt completely at a loss," Jackie recalls. "I remember thinking that it actually was a good thing that I had a Cesarean, because I got to stay there longer and get all that help."

At some point, Jackie, who under most circumstances is somewhat shy, gave up any attempt at modesty. Nursing two babies at once was hard enough. Trying to keep a blanket over both of them felt impossible. "People who came to visit me at the hospital room saw a lot more than they were expecting," she laughs. "Eventually I just left my gown off and pulled my sheets and blankets down to my waist. I didn't even bother trying to maneuver anything over my chest." She sighs at the memory. "I didn't see the point. The girls were pretty much latched on all the time."

It didn't take long before Jackie and her daughters were deemed healthy enough to leave the hospital. The family—now with twice as many members as it had the week before—gingerly packed themselves into the car and drove home. It was then, Jackie says, that her adventure really began.

"Once we got home, it was really, really hard," she says resignedly. "The entire experience was physically draining—which sounds silly, maybe, but nursing *is* literally draining several hundred calories a day out of your body." Jackie's husband had to go back to work almost immediately after the birth, and caring for two crying babies—by herself—left Jackie exhausted, lonely, and *starving*. There were some days when she felt like she literally didn't have time to grab herself something to eat until her husband came home.

Some nursing mothers find the lactating body's amazing calorie-burning capacity exhilarating, but for Jackie, the combination of hunger, sleep deprivation (the babies were eating on different schedules, waking and nursing every hour around the clock), and recovery from surgery was enough to make her feel drained and physically weak.

"During those first few weeks, it seemed like there was nothing I could do to help myself feel better," she says. "Everything was out of my hands. The loss of control was the weirdest thing about being a parent. I had a hard time accepting it. When I was pregnant, I knew there were things I could do to make it a good pregnancy, but after the babies were born and I was breastfeeding them, everything was up in the air. It felt to me like I had very little control over what my body was doing. There was no right answer, no secret key to make it all perfect. For me, the weeks after the babies were born felt like an extension of labor, a time when my body took over and I couldn't do anything about it."

This loss of control—combined with normal hormonal fluctuations and family stress—is what makes the postpartum period so difficult for new mothers. Dr. Swigart believes that few modern, educated women are prepared for just how carnal it is to breastfeed and care for a newborn. "Babies are like lovers—they demand physical love and caring in an intense, demanding, intimate way," she says. "For some women, this can feel like too much. Unless they learn to let go of some of the cerebral, they feel exhausted, depressed, and on edge."

Dr. Swigart's description fits Jackie to a T. "This was the first time in my life that my *physical* self was more important than my *mental* self," she says. "I had been in school for so long that thinking was what I did. It never even occurred to me that once I gave birth, my body would become so much more of who I was than my brain. That made me feel uneasy at the beginning, because I felt like I was just food for the babies, nothing else."

The further we get away from the days when women were perceived as doing little else but giving birth to and caring for their children, and the more we feel that we can control our own destinies, the harder the postpartum experience becomes. It's a sticky situation. The advances brought about by feminism have made life unquestionably better for women, but they have also taken us further away from our base nature, a reality we are confronted with when we bring a new life into the world. This is a conflict Dr. Swigart ran into when her own children were born. Many of her clients experience it, too.

"The earliest experiences we have with our children are so overwhelming, it is difficult to think clearly about them," Dr. Swigart writes in *The Myth of the Perfect Mother*. "The birth and care of an infant confounds the rational parts of ourselves, jolting us out of ordinary perceptions, catapulting us in and out of altered states." Babies, with all their burping, pooping, and crying, with their uninhibited ability to express their deepest joys and desires, sometimes remind people of their own inner needs and desires, Dr. Swigart says. Some mothers feel uncomfortable, because "uncensored" behavior cuts too close to the bone. They see in their babies things they're afraid of seeing in themselves.

Jackie knew that in order to regain her mental health, she needed to get out of the house—her family also needed another income. So four months after her daughters were born, she took a teaching job at a local community college. She was away from the house for only six hours a week, which turned out to be just the break she needed.

"It felt so good to get out of the house," Jackie sighs. "I was making all this milk, and I had to stuff my chest with tissues so I wouldn't leak everywhere, but it still felt really good to be out on my own for a few hours. I felt a little guilty at first, but then I got over it."

Jackie breastfed her daughters for more than half a year, a feat she now looks back on with pride. She knows her story is nothing exceptional: She's heard about mothers who've successfully nursed twins—or even triplets—for years, but from where she stands, seven months feels like a big accomplishment.

Through the Fire

Some mothers remember the first few weeks after a child's birth as a sentimental haze of diapers, excited grandparents, and soft newborn cuddles. Angie, a thirty-six-year-old home day-care provider, remembers her daughter's first days on the planet as a time of excruciating pain—and as an opportunity to develop a twisted new sense of humor.

"That first month, nursing was so painful," Angie recalls. "Every time she'd latch on, it was like fire. I'd want to scream and I couldn't, because I knew it would freak out the baby."

Under pressure, Angie's husband came up with a unique way to distract his wife from her tender breasts. "My husband and his friend like to play the guitar," Angie says, laughing at the memory. "One night this friend came over, and I was just sitting there rocking back and forth because my nipples hurt so much. They made up new words to the Johnny Cash song 'Ring of Fire,' something about how it hurt so damn much to nurse. In the end, I was laughing instead of crying. We tried to use humor as much as possible to get through the pain."

Two weeks into the ordeal, Angie and her daughter went to a lactation consultant to see if she could help them figure out what was going wrong. The consultant worked with the pair on perfecting their latch, and while she was at it, she examined Angie's breasts. There was some yellow crust on Angie's nipples, and the nurse swabbed it and sent it to the lab. It turned out she had an infection.

Nursing mothers are particularly vulnerable to bacterial infections, which can cause such common breastfeeding woes as mastitis (you can read more about this type of infection in later chapters) and sore, pus-oozing nipples. Depending on the type and severity of the infection, doctors commonly prescribe antibiotics in cream or oral form. Angie took a dose of pills, the infection cleared up, and slowly the pain began to lessen.

Because she never expected breastfeeding to be hard, Angie felt let down when it turned out to be. "There were times in the first few weeks when I didn't want to breastfeed because it hurt so bad," she says. "I remember sitting in the bathtub using warm water to massage my breasts to get them ready to feed her, and I was just crying. Part of it was the pain, another part was the disappointment."

You might wonder, Why didn't she just give up?

Truth is, she doesn't know. "I wasn't getting any pressure from my husband, but I still didn't want to let him down. I didn't want to let my daughter down, either, but there were times when I'd say to myself, 'I don't think I can do this anymore!'" she says. "Then I'd be back at myself with something like: 'I can't let her down. I chose to do this. I want to do this. I don't want to end it after just two weeks.'"

Somewhere inside, there was also a part of Angie that didn't want to let *Angie* down. "I planned on doing it way before she was born," she explains. "A lot of my friends had nursed, and I had read the information about how it's the best food for the baby. I think I would've felt like a failure if I gave up without really trying."

At some point—Angie can't pinpoint an exact date—breastfeeding stopped being a pain, both literally and figuratively. "We got into the groove somehow," she says. "It became easy and even pleasurable."

At fifteen months, Angie's toddler is still nursing. Neither mother nor daughter has plans to call it quits. "I think I'm gonna go with her as long as she wants," Angie says. "I don't want to cut her off. She's very attached to nursing, and she's not really demanding. I think I'm gonna go with her schedule and her needs and let her determine how long we continue. Plus, I put a lot of work into getting it established, so why would I want to quit now?"

As her daughter gets more active and talkative, Angie has noticed that some people seem uncomfortable when they realize that she is still breastfeeding.

"My mom and dad have asked me, 'How long do you think you're going to nurse her?'" Angie says. "Usually, I give them the same response I gave you, about how I'm going to let her make that decision. Sometimes, I'll hear friends saying something about people nursing a two-year-old and how they think that's gross. Either they know or they don't know I'm still nursing. I think it's strange that it bugs them, but I don't say anything in response to it. I don't have a philosophical point to make with it or anything. I'm doing it because it just feels right to me."

While Angie doesn't get involved in debates about the merits of breast versus bottle, she does try to offer advice and assistance to mothers who are struggling with nursing. She wants them to know that it was hard for her at the beginning, too, but it got better eventually, and that made everything worth it.

"We had some friends who just had a baby," Angie says, offering an example. "I remember before the baby was born, the mother said she was not going to breastfeed because she thought it was gross. Now it turns out she is nursing, but she's having a really hard time with it. I told her that the first two weeks are the hardest. If you stick it out for two weeks, it will get better. 'It won't be bad forever,' I said. 'I should know.'"

The Straight Dope

I feel like a tightrope walker. On one side of the wiggly wire on which I totter stands my steadfast belief that in all things, unflinching honesty is your best weapon against disappointment. On the other side is my heartfelt concern that too many horror stories about infection and screaming babies and bleeding, blistered nipples will push the faint of heart right off the fence into Formulaland. I don't want to do that.

Breastfeeding advocates like Deborah Dee tell me to back off a bit. They worry that too much honesty may not be a good thing.

"You walk a very fine line between trying to promote breast-feeding and being honest with women that breastfeeding may not be that smooth at the beginning," she says. "If you tell some women that, will it discourage them from even considering nursing in the first place? Somehow you need to make it clear that despite any struggles, breastfeeding is worth it in the end."

But I'm not good at keeping my mouth shut. And if you're anything like the women I know and love, you're tougher than most people give you credit for, especially when it comes to your children. You have been disappointed before and you've lived to tell the tale—maybe even hilariously—to your friends and relatives. Best of all, you understand that life is rarely perfect, and despite what you've been led to believe, a little clearheaded hard work usually pays off with amazing rewards.

It's sort of like sex: If you go into it thinking that everything will be soft-focus and choreographed, like the airbrushed *luv*making depicted on daytime TV, you're bound to come crashing down to earth the first time you discover that real-life dalliances can be sweaty and awkward and even heartbreaking. What you learn later is that sweaty, awkward, heartbreaking sex can be the best (read: nastiest, earthiest, *realest*) kind of all, much closer to true love than anything you'll ever see on *The Bachelorette*. And once you accept—and even embrace—life's imperfections, your load will be that much lighter.

So, I don't want any of you to go into this breastfeeding thing innocently, armed with nothing but sappy stories and childhood fantasies about how wonderful and blissful and natural it will feel to feed your baby. I don't want you to think of yourself as a failure if it's tougher than you imagined or if you eventually throw in the towel and pick up a can of formula. Once you come to accept the fact that nursing—and by extension, motherhood—is a sweaty, awkward, heartbreaking undertaking, you'll begin to find the deep joy and pleasure in it, to understand why women keep having babies, even though babies can be a real pain in the ass.

But—and here's the big *but* that I drag around with me everywhere—I don't want you to think that nursing is always a difficult experience. Some women, like Liz, a thirty-five-year-old stay-at-home mom from Arlington, Massachusetts, find it remarkably effortless from the very beginning. Both of her children, a boy and girl born about three and one-half years apart, latched on immediately—and correctly—right after their births.

"I was really lucky," Liz admits, almost sheepishly. "It's like they were showing *me* how to do it." Both of her kids breastfed enthusiastically, and Liz never suffered from breast infections or sore nipples or any of the other maladies I've been busy scaring you with so far.

Even so, Liz isn't one to brag. She continues to insist that when it comes to nursing, she was just born lucky, biologically speaking. "I don't have any preexisting physical problems with my breasts, like inverted nipples or surgeries," she says. "I also have relatively dark skin, and that helps. I've heard that people with really light skin tend to have more nipple tenderness. I never had blisters or anything. I have this pale, red-haired friend and she got cracked nipples right away."

Part of Liz's success might also be chalked up to her attitude and social situation. Her mother, a La Leche League activist, breastfed her until she was more than three years old, and when her oldest child was born, Liz—with the support of her husband and her extended family—chose to stay home full-time and focus on motherhood.

Liz found that relaxing and just letting the mamatide pull her in helped make breastfeeding easier, too. She was at home all the time, so she never felt the need to put her kids on a formal schedule. Because she didn't have to rush out the door and go to work each morning, for instance, she could spend as much time as she wanted just nursing her children.

Before you start rolling your eyes at Liz's mellow mamastyle, understand that she's the first to admit that her willingness to put the rest of her life on hold for her children doesn't—and shouldn't—work for everyone. She's not trying to get all up in your face, preaching some self-righteous "megamom" approach to parenthood. It's just what worked for her.

Staying home full-time isn't the only way to make nursing easy. Sometimes biology, attitude, and dumb luck intersect, and your baby takes to the breast so naturally that he practically teaches *you* how to nurse. Take Laura, the daily-newspaper columnist and mother of two. To say she had a difficult time giving birth to her first baby would be putting it lightly. After twelve hours of labor, Laura pushed for hours before doctors decided that the baby just wouldn't fit through her pelvis. She needed to undergo an emergency C-section. After such an exhausting, traumatic birth, Laura wouldn't have been surprised if breastfeeding was difficult, too, but her not-so-little boy (he tipped the scales at almost ten pounds) proved himself a nursing pro from the first time she placed him on her breast.

"I think I've got the kind of nipples that are shaped just right for the job," Laura chuckles. "Before I had children, I never really liked my boobs. I always wanted a set of those perky, gravity-defying ones, but now that I have kids, I realize that my breasts are de-signed for function, not form. Since I started breastfeeding, I've developed a whole new appreciation of my body and what it's ca-pable of doing."

Ultimately, if you've been having difficulty, sticking it out can be incredibly gratifying. Once it works, there's nothing better. Tina is the forty-year-old development director from Minneapolis. A little more than three months after her daughter's birth, Tina's little girl (who'd been born at twenty-six weeks gestation) was discharged from the hospital, and though she was doing just fine in most re-gards, she still hadn't developed a strong-enough sucking impulse to feed directly from her mother's breast. Determined to give her daughter the best possible food, Tina pumped breast milk and fed it to her from a bottle, but the routine of *pump-feed-pump-feed* was getting exhausting.

Then, only a few weeks after this wonder baby came home from the hospital, something startling happened. "I had just given her a bottle," Tina recalls. "I put her down in her crib while I went to pump, and suddenly she started crying her hungry cry. I was fed up, so I put her to my breast—I'd been doing that for weeks with no success—but for some unknown reason, she suddenly latched on. She never went back."

Tina says she has no way of knowing why that one last try clicked for her baby, but it did. She may never know, but when it finally happened, it was like suddenly all those hours spent in the hospital, all the tears and worry over her little girl, had paid off with this one little accomplishment. For that moment, anyway, she could set the past aside and move forward.

"I don't know why I didn't give up," Tina says. "I can't put that into words. It was just some sort of feeling of inner resolve. In the hospital and later on, there were times when I would think, 'I'm gonna stop this madness,' but then I'd keep doing it. The amazing thing is that something that was such a source of stress and tension has turned into this satisfying experience. It tested my strength, and in the end I feel even stronger because of it."

The Mama Advisory Board on Getting Started

- **"Be patient,"** says Maja. "I swear breastfeeding gets better eventually. It can feel impossible at the beginning, but *it will get better.*"
- **Find yourself a breastfeeding mentor,** advises Ola. "My mother-in-law nursed her kids, and her advice really helped me through the rough spots. I didn't know anything about how to do it before, so I don't know what I would've done without her."
- **Take advantage of any help you can get while you're still in the hospital,** says Jackie. And stay there for as long as you can—even if they seem ready to throw you out. "Talk to the nurses, see the hospital lactation consultant. Make sure you understand the basics of breastfeeding before you leave the hospital."
- **Don't be too tough.** Nursing *can* be a little painful at first, but Angie cautions that extreme pain can be a sign of trouble: "If it hurts so much it brings tears to your eyes, if it's not getting better, get yourself checked out."
- **Don't forget to eat**—especially if you're nursing twins. Jackie suggests setting up a high-carb snack station on your bedside table, with apples, crackers, bagels, bananas, and water. "I burned so many calories at the beginning when I was nursing my babies around the clock. I really couldn't eat enough. If I didn't snack all the time, I'd feel weak and tired by the end of the day."

Chapter 2

Dump the Guilt, Not the Milk

You heard it here first: There's no RIGHT way to be a mother. This includes what you do with your breasts

A n attorney for a large multinational corporation, Barbara has a firm, professional handshake. She wears a simple pant-suit, very little makeup, and plain, round glasses. This self-described "glamorous combination of lawyer and earth mother" is the high-achieving, oldest daughter of a crunchy-Catholic mother, a woman who went to church every Sunday, baked her own bread, and regularly attended La Leche League meetings. "I like to tell people my mom's a hippie with morals," Barbara jokes.

As a young teen growing up in Sioux Falls, South Dakota, Barbara had watched her mother nurse her much younger sister. The older woman's devotion to the production and distribution of mother's milk made a big impression on her. While über-professional Barbara may not have aspired to replicate everything about her stay-at-home mother's life, she always thought that when it came to raising babies, she would do things pretty much like Mom did: natural childbirth, homemade baby food, cloth diapers, and, of course, exclusive breast-feeding. "I had this image of myself," Barbara says. "I told everyone

I knew that I'd breastfeed for at least six months—though I really intended to do it for a year. From that perspective, at least, I was going to be just like my mom."

And at first it looked like she would. Barbara sailed through an easy, enviable pregnancy. "I wasn't sick," she says, her smile betraying just a hint of pride. "I looked good. I had this great birth with no drugs. I met all my early goals, and with that I just expected that breastfeeding would go smoothly."

But it didn't. While mother and child were still in the hospital, it seemed like Barbara's new baby had figured out nursing right away. But as it turns out, the baby wasn't latching correctly, and as soon as they got home, the problem only got worse. Sure, her sweet little girl was gaining weight (a good thing, by any mother's standards), but *Barbara* was in serious pain. Not just an annoying little ouch, but rather a teeth-gritting, eye-watering, this-hurts-like-hell kind of pain.

"Every time the baby would cry for food, I'd feel resentful," Barbara admits. "Then I'd feel horribly guilty about being resentful of feeding my baby. It was what you'd call a vicious cycle."

Barbara is one of those women (calling herself a "type-A achiever") who, once she sets a goal for herself, can get pretty fixated on it. During the first few days after she and her husband brought their daughter home from the hospital, the pain in Barbara's breasts continued to get worse. The baby, like newborns are wont to do, was eating pretty much nonstop.

I won't deny that for many women, myself included, breastfeeding hurts quite a bit at the beginning. While your nipples are busy toughening themselves up for the long road ahead, you may experience some minor cracking and even scabbing (yuck!), but that gnarly stuff should begin to heal itself after the first few days. If things start to get worse, get thee to a doctor or—even better—a lactation consultant, because nursing through extreme pain can be a recipe for trouble.

Breastfeeding experts explain that although a newborn infant may be able to get enough milk from just "chewing" on the end of the nipple—which was what it turned out Barbara's baby was doing—

if the infant doesn't bring the entire nipple and most of the areola into her mouth for nursing, the mother is at risk for a whole host of nasty maladies. Severe, unending pain—the eye-watering, teeth-gnashing variety—is your body's way of signaling that something isn't right. Sure enough, a few days after her daughter was born, Barbara's nipples began to crack and bleed. A week went by and then two. Things weren't getting any better. Barbara's left nipple was in the worst shape.

"One of the cracks just kept getting deeper and deeper," Barbara winces, illustrating the size of the wound by holding up her thumb and forefinger and squinting at the space between them. "We're talking *millimeters* deep here. It was no longer just a crack. It was a fissure, and it was so deep that I remember wondering if a person's nipple could actually fall off."

When Barbara finally ventured out of the house for a post-partum appointment at her ob-gyn's office, the nurse-practitioner took one look at Barbara's nipples and told her that she would have to wean the baby off her left breast. If she didn't, the nipple might never heal, and with a large open sore in an area regularly exposed to bacteria, Barbara was at risk for developing a serious infection. She could continue to feed her daughter from her right breast, the nurse continued, but Barbara would likely have to supplement with formula. She arranged for her to meet with a lactation consultant that same day.

"While she was telling me this, I just sat there in the office and cried," Barbara says. "She was saying that my perfect little girl was going to have to drink formula—*the devil's liquor.* She was saying that I'd have to wean on one side and become the Hunchboob of Notre Dame. I wasn't sure if I could do it. I felt guilty. And I felt awful."

We mamas are a well-meaning bunch, though with all our lofty goals and heady ambitions, many of us set ourselves up for disappointment, for opportunities to beat ourselves over the head for supposed "failures," like Barbara's "Hunchboob" breakdown.

"In this country, we tend to invest motherhood and breastfeeding with all this moral significance," says Linda Blum, PhD, professor of sociology at the University of New Hampshire in Durham and author of *At the Breast: Ideologies of Breastfeeding and Motherhood in the Contemporary United States.* "For many modern women, it's such a loaded experience. Our cultural expectations about what it takes to be the ideal mother make it almost impossible for us to do exactly right by our children. Many mothers find themselves butting up against those expectations in ways they never anticipated."

I know just how Barbara felt. In the weeks after my daughter's birth, I may have seemed to the outside world like I was handling everything just fine, but at the core, I never really felt like I was doing quite right by my sweet baby. Sure, I was nursing her and she was growing and thriving, but why did it take her so long to figure out how to latch on correctly? Wasn't I doing everything by the book? Why did I feel so tied down by the care and feeding of my demanding little nursling? And, most important: Why did I feel so damn guilty about everything?

Lactation consultant Catherine Adeboye, RN, IBCLC, says that she meets all kinds of women during her daily rounds in the maternity ward at Regions Hospital in St. Paul, Minnesota. High-achieving women, women who have read all the books on parenting and who have absorbed all available wisdom about what it takes to be a good mother, are often the ones who feel the worst when things don't work out perfectly from the start.

"We often run across these women who are used to having control over their lives," she says. "When the baby comes and they suddenly realize that they are not going to have control over this enormous part of their lives, say when breastfeeding turns out to be a bigger challenge than they anticipated, the rug gets pulled out from under them for a little while. Having a baby is a big transition for anyone. You can read about it all you want beforehand, but when it happens, many people still feel like they've just been tossed into the fire."

Adeboye and her colleagues—her large, urban hospital employs four board-certified lactation consultants—try to take an anti-guilt approach to their work with new breastfeeding mothers. "We think of it as our job to work with each mother to find an approach that works best for her," she says. "While it's certainly our job to encourage breastfeeding—we believe it's best for the baby and the mother—we also want to make it a positive experience for everyone involved. Throwing guilt around, making women feel like failures if nursing doesn't work for them, is counterproductive. We want mothers to be proud of their accomplishments, whatever form they take."

Barbara had always demanded the best from herself, and when breastfeeding didn't work the way she planned, it was a major letdown. When it became clear that she would need to get help—in the form of formula—to keep both herself and her daughter healthy, the nurse's orders bounced around in her postpartum brain until they took on the weight of tragedy.

"I hadn't been faced with a lot of failure in my life," Barbara says. "Even when I was a kid, I'd always set a goal and then I'd achieve it. This felt like a pretty significant thing to fail at."

Her guilt-brain at the boiling point, Barbara went home and picked up the phone.

"I was sad and feeling pretty desperate," she recalls. "I called my mom and told her about what was going on. She said, 'Are you thinking about quitting?' I took a deep breath and said, 'Yeah.' She said, 'It's okay, you know.' That's really all I needed to hear. It was like I had her blessing. I finally had permission to stop, and for some reason, that permission is what ultimately gave me the strength to keep going."

In the end, Barbara's worst dreams were not realized. After a few early struggles, she successfully weaned on her left side, and continued to breastfeed her daughter on the right—with supplemental formula—until she was a year old. And her own mother—the fervent nursing advocate—turned out to be her biggest supporter.

One day, when Barbara's mother was visiting her new

granddaughter, a family friend came to visit. "This friend was a nurse. This was when I was weaning my daughter off one breast, and I was giving her a bottle of formula. This friend looked at me and then my mom in a significant way and said, 'Oh, so you're giving your baby a *bottle?*' As soon as the words came out of the friend's mouth, Mom's mama bear side appeared. She said sternly, 'Barbara's had a lot of problems. She's doing a great job.' End of discussion."

Nearly losing a nipple helped Barbara develop a more relaxed attitude about motherhood. She realized that when it comes to being a parent, perfection is an overrated goal. At some core level, she came to understand that there are just some things—like her baby or her body, or her life, for that matter—that she just can't control. The end result was a deeper understanding of the whole unpredictable motherhood thing, and a grudging ability to let go of some of the guilt.

As a mother, you may often feel that the key ingredients that make up a happy life—like time, patience, and a ready sense of humor—are in short supply. But somehow most mothers never have to worry about having enough guilt to go around. There's always some way we don't measure up, can't perform, fall short of the high expectations we set for ourselves. At some point, most of us learn that we have to get a grip, for godsakes, and slowly, layer by tissue-thin layer, we begin to peel the guilt away. The process can be painful, but in the end we reveal our stronger, more confident cores.

"What I learned along the way was that I am a good mom," says Barbara. "My baby would still love me if I gave her formula and is so beautiful that I am amazed that she is related to me. My mother would love me if I gave my baby formula. My sister, who didn't wean her son until he was two, would still love me, too. Rationally, I knew that people would still love me if I stopped nursing, but in the thick of it, I truly did worry about stupid stuff like that. Now I realize that it wasn't this major failure, but at the time, I felt like I really was letting everybody down. I now know that next time, I'm going to have to lower my expectations."

The Milk Mafia

A few years ago, Beth, a thirty-eight-year-old editor for a Minneapolis alternative newsweekly, wrote an article about her struggles learning to breastfeed her first child—a healthy-but-sleepy jaundiced boy. The article touched on Beth's own feelings of inadequacy, on the exhausting first days home from the hospital, and on her worries over whether she'd ever be a "good enough" mother. She also wrote about returning to work, about pumping, about public nursing, about lactation history, and about what she saw as the "conspiracy of guilt and silence" that surrounds American breastfeeding culture. Beth had been writing for nearly fifteen years, and though she's never shied away from controversial topics, she was caught off-guard by the reaction to this particular article.

"After that story came out, I received the most hate mail that I ever got in my writing career," Beth says. "It was all from women, too! I had people writing that I should be sterilized, that my children should be taken away, that I was a horrible mother. And I *breastfed.* It was like by writing about my own ambivalence, I had criticized all women who had managed to breastfeed exclusively. People were reacting like I had called them dirty names. I was flabbergasted by the amount of guilt that was flying around."

There were times when Beth felt that by honestly expressing her doubts about—and struggles with—breastfeeding, she'd stepped on a land mine. It was as if many readers didn't want to hear a mother say publicly that nursing was hard. And they certainly didn't want her to talk about sending her child to day care—or about slipping him the occasional bottle of formula.

"The whole thing's a setup," Beth snorts. "There's no way that you can feel about the topic that's not gonna trip a wire." The judgment comes from both sides of the debate. Many people still think that breastfeeding beyond six months or a year equals overindulgence. Some even think it's a sign of sexually inappropriate behavior. People on the other end of the spectrum go so far as to say that formula-feeding is a form of child abuse.

"The guilt is there. The blame is there," Beth says. "I'd just like us to get to the point where we quit judging each other—and ourselves. Clearly, there's way too much baggage attached to this breastfeeding thing."

Dr. Blum's book, *At the Breast,* attracted its share of controversy, too. An academic investigation of American attitudes about breastfeeding and motherhood combined with an analysis of current medical research, the book suggests that the strident, militant tone of modern breastfeeding advocacy actually *divides* women, making for polarized groups of "good" and "bad" mothers separated in large part by race, education, and economic status. Dr. Blum argues that a woman's ability or willingness to breastfeed beyond the first few weeks of a child's life often depends on whether she works outside of the home, whether she has adequate emotional or economic support, and whether she has been educated about the benefits of nursing. While studies highlighting breastfeeding's benefits have been widely reported, Dr. Blum asserts that in the Western world, some of the health and developmental advantages claimed for breastfed babies— like higher IQs, stronger immune systems, and decreased risk of serious childhood illnesses like asthma and diabetes—may be due more to social advantage than to mothers' milk.

"In a society like ours that has so much inequality, breastfeeding is very much determined by social position," she explains. "When comparing breastfeeding and nonbreastfeeding groups, it may be impossible to tease out whether a difference in the overall health or development of a group of children is due to breastfeeding or to other environmental or social factors."

For good reason, breastfeeding advocates take exception to Dr. Blum's arguments. (Dr. Blum herself will tell you that in some communities, her sociologist's interpretation of medical research has made her a pariah.) "I don't know what you achieve when you minimize the advantages of breastfeeding for any group of mothers," says Adeboye. "For all children across the board, the advantages to breastfeeding are clear, but maybe it makes more sense to talk about the *disadvantages* of formula. If someone gives you the standard pro-breastfeeding talk, you'll hear things like 'Your child is less likely to get ear infections. Your child will have fewer allergies.' That's a nice way of putting it. But a more honest way of saying it is, 'If you formulafeed, your child has an *increased risk* of ear infections. If you formulafeed, your child has an *increased risk* of diabetes.' What's correct is that there are risks to formulafeeding, and mothers should be aware of that."

Dr. Blum insists that despite her controversial analysis, she continues to believe that breastfeeding is best for mothers and children. She is vocal in her support for breastfeeding advocacy groups like La Leche League and is interested in campaigns designed to make nursing a realistic option for women of all social classes. But that reality rarely silences her critics.

"People don't want to have their assumptions questioned," Dr. Blum says. "But by holding the breastfeeding mother up as the cultural ideal, I think we've put way too much pressure on all mothers. We've drawn a line that separates us from each other. An over-stressed mother or a mother with insecure housing is much more dangerous to a child's well-being than a mother who feeds formula to her infant."

The Truth Shall Set You Free

In her former life as a TV producer, thirty-two-year-old Allison was no stranger to hard work. At a relatively young age, she'd made a name for herself in Washington State broadcasting, working long hours under tight deadlines to earn the respect of her colleagues. But after her son was born and she began what she calls her "second career" as a stay-at-home mom, Allison discovered that the hardest work of her life was still ahead of her.

"I know it's a cliché, but there are just so many challenges to raising a kid," Allison says. "Before I actually started doing it, I thought that by being home I would have so much control over everything—but I quickly found out that I didn't."

For Allison, the first control-buster was nursing.

"Before my son was born, I took a four-hour breastfeeding course at the hospital where we decided to give birth," she says. "I came out of there thinking that breastfeeding was just like what you read about or see on TV, where as soon as the baby's born, you pop him on, he's nursing, and that's the end of it."

In many ways, that *was* the end of it. From the beginning, Allison's baby latched well. He grew steadily and quickly, plumping up into one of those smiling butterball babies that make even complete strangers smile.

"I didn't have mastitis, I didn't have cracked or bleeding nipples," Allison admits, with the slightest hint of embarrassment. "From the outside, anyhow, it probably seemed like things were going very well." But from Allison's perspective, things weren't going well at all.

"At the beginning, nursing felt like an unpleasant chore," she recalls. "It was really uncomfortable, even painful. My nipples were amazingly sore. To put it lightly, it wasn't something that I looked forward to. Plus, at first the baby nursed for a really long time. I would sit there for forty-five minutes to an hour, and then I'd have to change his diaper, and before you knew it, I had to start over again. It felt like I was always nursing him."

None of this is unusual. Newborns often nurse almost continuously, and at the beginning, many—if not most—mothers complain of sore nipples, a malady that usually fades after a few weeks of just muscling through. Allison was committed to breastfeeding and determined to stick it out, but as the first weeks threatened to turn into months, she realized that her classic new-mother emotions like awe and confusion were turning into something that felt a lot more like frustration. She felt annoyed about nursing, guilty about feeling annoyed, and angry that nobody had told her that breastfeeding her baby would be hard.

When she thought back to her hospital's breastfeeding class—and she did that often during those first few weeks—she got angry when she realized that this would have been the perfect opportunity for somebody, *anybody,* to tell the roomful of participants the truth, as Allison saw it: "that breastfeeding isn't always a bed of roses, but eventually it will get better." If someone would've just leveled with her at the beginning, Allison reasoned, maybe she wouldn't feel like such a freak now.

"I knew that, in reality, I didn't have much to complain about," she says. "But I felt like complaining." Each time she did—to her mother or her husband or her sister—she felt sheepish and guilty.

Allison and her husband live in a comfortable house in suburban Seattle. Her "extremely, totally earthy" hospital (the maternity ward doesn't allow disposable diapers, for instance) offered a weekly support group for new parents. Allison, who was looking for ways to get out of the house, signed up immediately. "In the group, there were definitely women who got sideways glances when they gave their babies bottles," she recalls, adding that in her community, formula-feeding is the exception to the rule. Most babies she knows start—and stay—at the breast. "In the group, there was definitely a militant vibe going on," Allison continues. "The moms there were so into breastfeeding that I imagine that anyone who wasn't doing it might have felt very judged."

Looking back, Allison admits that her read on the support group's militant vibe may have been influenced by her own feelings of guilt about not grooving on breastfeeding as much as the other mothers seemed to be. She wanted to be a supermom—she had quit her job to take care of her son, after all—and here she was, feeling frustrated by the most basic part of mothering. Ever the researcher, Allison had read every breastfeeding guide she could lay her hands on, but the only nursing mothers she read about were the blissful, semi-orgasmic types. None of the women in the books—or in her parents' group, for that matter—seemed to feel as conflicted about the whole nursing thing as she did.

"So here we are" (by *we*, Allison means herself and Baby), "in the group, and about two months into it I'm still struggling with nursing. It was still painful, plus I felt like I was still doing it all the time. Finally, one day I burst out and said, 'Does anybody else here hate breastfeeding as much as I do?' There was this dead, painful silence, and then slowly a few people started saying, 'I hate it too,' or 'It's really hard,' or 'It's definitely been a struggle.' I think it took me speaking out to get them all beyond the 'It's beautiful and wonderful' scenario."

Hardly anybody is brave enough to question the popular notion that breastfeeding is in every case a pleasant, easy experience, Allison says. Nobody wants to admit that it can be hard at first. It's almost as though if they actually tell the truth—that nursing can be tough at first but it's definitely worth it—few women will be brave enough to do it.

A month or so later, after she and her son finally got breast-feeding figured out, Allison was asked to sit on a nursing mothers' panel at her hospital's breastfeeding-education class—the same class she and her husband had attended all those months before.

"I looked around the room, and here were all these pregnant women, many of them getting their first real education about breast-feeding," Allison recalls. "When it came time for me to speak, I knew this was my chance to set the record straight. I said, 'It was a struggle. I'm glad I stuck with it, but don't think that breastfeeding is necessarily going to be this really euphoric experience. I was any-thing but euphoric for the first three months.'" Allison chuckles at the memory and continues, "The instructor jumped in, and in front of all the people attending the class, she said, 'You mean three *weeks*,' and then moved on before I could explain that no, I really did mean three *months*."

For Allison, sitting on the mothers' panel felt like starring in an episode of *The Twilight Zone*. "Here I was with these other women who were talking about how nursing was this amazing endorphic ex-perience, and all the time I was thinking, 'These women are crazy!' They are creating really false expectations for these pregnant women. I felt like I needed to speak out because everyone else seemed afraid to."

And once she began speaking up, Allison hasn't stopped. As part of her own personal campaign to reduce the guilt, to spread the word that breastfeeding is a tough job that takes time and patience, Allison will tell her story to any soon-to-be nursing mother who's willing to listen.

"I'm not trying to scare them away," she insists. "But I also want them to know that they're not crazy or a bad mother if they think it's hard. It's one of the hardest things you'll ever do. But it's also one of the best."

The Invisible Mom

In Allison's part of the country, it's not uncommon to see mothers breastfeeding talkative toddlers in coffee shops, or to read articles about citywide nurse-ins. But in the heart of Manhattan, committed, long-term breastfeeders are almost as rare as dodo birds. Or at least that's the perception of Janelle, a thirty-six-year-old sales director from New York City.

Janelle moved to New York from her native Wisconsin over a decade ago. She always knew that she wanted to have a family someday—she and her husband even purchased a house with room for children just outside of the city—but she waited until she reached a stable place in her career before trying to have a baby. When she gave birth to her daughter, Janelle set out to construct a life that made room for both a family *and* a career. She never planned on quitting her job—or even reducing her hours—after the baby was born.

From the start, Janelle planned on nursing her little girl, and though she had a fairly easy time of it, she says she never felt determined to be "a full-time milk machine." Plus, even though she knew all about pumping and the flexibility it gives many employed mothers, she wasn't convinced that nursing and a demanding job were compatible. "I love my daughter, but I also love my job," Janelle says. "I wanted to do what was best for both."

A few weeks into her three-month maternity leave, Janelle discovered that the steady routine of caring for a newborn was already losing its luster. Safely ensconced in her suburban house, she missed her job in the city, interacting with her coworkers, closing deals, and meeting with clients. While her daughter was delightful, she wasn't exactly *company,* and sitting around the house ("at first, I felt like I hardly ever left the couch," Janelle sighs) all day wasn't enough to keep Janelle's normally active mind from feeling like it was atrophying. Part of her wanted *out,* and though she knew some people somewhere might judge her desires, the truth was she didn't feel all that guilty about them. She was a good mother—she was convinced of that—but she also knew what was best for *her.* Nursing, Janelle decided, had become emblematic of her life with a new baby. It was repetitive, slow, and brainless: In other words, it was stupefying.

"I was getting bored by the sameness of it all," Janelle admits. "I was definitely not the kind of mother who was like, 'Oh, I *love* breastfeeding.' It was more something I had to do. At the beginning, I didn't love the concept of being tied to the whole damn schedule of feeding every two, three hours. Everything you do seems to revolve around that next feeding. Sure, I knew I was going to do it because it was the best thing for my daughter, but I was also going to set an end-date for myself."

Brave words for a woman who lives in a society that to some degree still harbors the belief that the best mothers are those who are willing to give up everything (i.e., career, social life, even emotional and physical health) for their babies. Any mother gutsy enough to profess her *unwillingness* to do so sets herself up for some pretty harsh criticism. But Janelle's no shrinking violet. She knows what she needs in order to be a healthy human being, and, by extension, a good mom.

When we establish the paragon of the selfless mother, the woman who slowly shrinks into the shadow of her needy child, we lay a trap for mothers who can't or won't fit into this mold. (And the truth is that, to some degree, that's most of us.) The guilt of not measuring up to the cultural ideal, of not doing the right thing, whatever the right thing may be, forces mothers to see their choices in terms of black or white, rather than in shades of gray. The mother who enjoys her job and takes her child to day care becomes a *heartless career woman;* the mother who quits it all to stay at home with the kids becomes a *dumpy housewife.* In either scenario, the woman be-hind the stereotype all but disappears, and we end up establishing distinct, separate camps based on our childrearing choices—and little else.

Biding her time at home, Janelle was torn about when was the right time for her to begin to wean her daughter. Then, when the baby was about six weeks old, Janelle developed a blister on one of her nipples, and the question answered itself.

"One night I was watching TV. I was feeling a little tired and achy like I had the flu, and ten minutes later I had a fever of 104," Janelle recalls. "It turns out it was mastitis, but at the time I thought I was dying. It comes on that fast. My breasts were swollen, and it felt like I was carrying around twenty pounds on the front of me." Concerned, Janelle called her hospital's breastfeeding hotline.

"I told the woman who answered the phone that I had a high fever. I said I thought maybe I had mastitis," Janelle recalls. "The first thing out of her mouth was, 'DO NOT STOP BREASTFEEDING!' Her voice was totally high and panicked. She said, 'You *have* to nurse through it.' I said, 'What about *me*? I'm totally sick here.' And then she was like, quickly, 'Oh yeah, you should call your doctor and get an antibiotic.'"

To Janelle, it felt like the woman on the hotline had it backward. "She was afraid of losing me, like I was going to fall from the ranks of breastfeeding mothers, and my daughter wasn't going to get the holy mother's milk." Janelle says that while the woman on the other end of the phone was justified in her concern for Janelle's infant daughter, what she should have been most concerned about was the stress that this incredible life change was causing for *Janelle,* about how this painful infection threatened to push her beyond simple am-bivalence about nursing to actual distaste.

Janelle got a prescription for an antibiotic, and after a few days the mastitis faded, but by that time, any appeal breastfeeding held for her was gone. She weaned her daughter at fourteen weeks, coin-ciding very closely with her return to work.

Janelle was more than ready to be done with this chapter in her life. She felt like she'd exceeded her own personal minimum goal of six weeks, and that with her help, her baby had had the best possible start in life. When she felt like she was being "guilted" into nursing, she threw in the towel.

"It was like the health professionals weren't really concerned about my health," Janelle says, looking back on the experience. "They were too wrapped up in the cult of breastfeeding to really pay attention to what was going on in my brain. When I realized that, I started seeing that attitude more and more. In the end, when I stopped nursing, I really didn't feel guilty at all. I felt like I did the best that I could do—plus I kept my sanity."

Grandma Made Me Do It

I care way too much about what other people think. It gets in my way, this impulse to please others, makes me a horrible waitress, a nervous hostess, and—at the beginning, at least—a supershy breast-feeder. I know now that nursing doesn't have to look anything like a striptease (unless that's what the mother wants it to resemble), but when my daughter was tiny, the thought of feeding her in public made me freeze with fear.

I was deathly afraid that I'd have the baby latched on and someone would (loudly) object. Soon everyone would see what was going on, and I'd have to spend the rest of my life wearing a scarlet *B* (for breastfeeder) pinned to my chest.

These days, though I still care what other people think about my writing, or the way I raise my children, or the shade of my lipstick, and though I'd still make a pretty *crap*tacular waitress, I have loosened up quite a bit on the breastfeeding front. (I'd even wear a scarlet *B* with pride.) I've nursed in some pretty public venues, but there are still a few places where and a few people (dad, father-in-law, male coworkers, to name a few) in front of whom I'm still not willing to whip 'em out. Call me uptight, but I'm just not ready to face the discomfort, the implied disapproval. Tits out, I feel vulnerable to criticism.

That's why I've always admired women like Liz, the thirty-five-year-old stay-at-home mom from Arlington, Massachusetts, who boldly breastfed her babies well past babyhood and into toddlerdom. For two years, Liz and her oldest child, a son, shared a common love of nursing.

"We both just really enjoyed it," Liz recalls. "Although I had my share of challenges with parenthood and being a mom, it turns out that breastfeeding is one thing I am pretty good at. For the two of us, it was a real bonding experience and something that we were in no rush to stop."

Because it was so easy and convenient, Liz was still nursing on demand as her son neared his second birthday. Liz's own mother had nursed her until she was almost three years old, and Liz felt good about passing on this family tradition of childrearing. But as her son got closer to the two-year mark, the romance of nursing began to wear thin. For one thing, Liz was considering getting pregnant again. And out of nowhere, she was starting to feel self-conscious about breastfeeding her active, verbal son in public.

"I never thought I'd feel that way," Liz admits, "but at a certain point, I developed an irrational fear that somebody would think what we were doing was wrong and give me an evil look. I just couldn't handle that."

Then Great-Grandma weighed in with her opinion. Liz and her son were at the retirement community on their weekly visit. When Liz's toddler ran over, jumped up on his mother's lap, and began to nurse, Grandma smiled stiffly and asked, "How long are you going to do this?" Liz giggles at the memory, gently mimicking her grandmother's voice: "'In my apartment you can do what you want, but you can't nurse him downstairs in the common room.' That's my grandmother's style. No subtlety."

Even though Liz felt angry about the way the message was delivered, she honored her grandmother's request and kept her nursing sessions to the apartment. Her grandmother had never nursed her own children, and though she'd been outwardly supportive of Liz's parenting decisions, clearly she felt that her granddaughter had reached a point where public breastfeeding had become unacceptable. "My grandma tends to think that what *she* did was right," Liz explains.

Though she hates to admit it, Liz believes that her grandmother's squeamishness played a role in her decision to wean her son. She'd already been wondering if nursing had grown beyond nutrition or comfort and turned more into a habit. "I like to think of myself as the sort of person who doesn't care too much what other people think," she says. "But I was already feeling on the fence, and this just pushed me over."

Liz began by telling her son that they would now only nurse at home. She drew a picture illustrating the times when they could nurse and talked to him about things that they could do instead of nursing, like singing a song or hugging or holding hands. Her son easily accepted these new conditions, and Liz discovered that she felt relieved. "It was nice to not have that immediate reaction of always whipping out a boob every time he was upset," she laughs. "It was nice to find other ways to comfort him."

The weaning progressed in that way, with Liz's son nursing only in the morning and at night before bed, and then slowly asking for the breast less and less, until one day he just stopped. As the final day approached, Liz felt torn between joy at having her freedom back and sorrow at losing this key connection with her son. She felt guilty for stopping, and sometimes in the darkest recesses of her mind, she also felt guilty for nursing him as long as she had.

"Sometimes the thought would cross my mind that it is weird for a boy to be nursing at this age," Liz says. "When he started seeming more like a child and less like a baby, sometimes it would seem jarring to me. And then when he was old enough to ask, to say, 'Nurse!' and be demanding, that started to get to me. I wanted my privacy, and I didn't want to be demanded of in that way. But I also knew that this was crap. I wanted to be there for him, and I hated to refuse this most basic thing."

San Francisco psychotherapist and author Jane Swigart, PhD, explains that breastfeeding mothers are often caught in such a double bind. "There are times when we wonder if what feels like the best thing for us will also be the best thing for our children," she says. "Eventually, freedom—in the form of weaning—may be essential for a mother's mental health, but it can be a gut-wrenching, guilt-inducing experience."

Ultimately, for Liz, breastfeeding became more of a chore than a joy. And while she felt wistful when her son finally hung up his milk hat for good, she also felt a flood of relief. By that time, she was pregnant again, and she looked forward to a few months of "having at least one part of my body back to myself."

By the time Liz's daughter was born, her son had been off the breast for six months. At the beginning, she worried about what he'd think when he saw this new kid moving in on his territory. It turns out that her concerns were groundless.

"The first time he saw me nursing my daughter, he looked sort of confused and maybe even a little bit grossed out," Liz laughs. "My impression is that he doesn't remember it at all. I think he considers himself way too mature for that kind of behavior."

Birth of a Lactivist

Back when she was pregnant, Marta, a 34-year-old stay-at-home mother from Austin, Texas, knew intellectually that breastfeeding was the best thing for her child, but she wasn't sure that she would actually be able to stick with it once her baby was born. She was adopted as an infant and had no siblings. Her mother-in-law didn't breastfeed. Neither did her grandmother. None of her close friends had babies yet, so she had no experience seeing other mothers succeed at nursing. She wasn't sure if she could, either.

"I had read all the books about how good breast milk is for babies, and I wanted to nurse my child, but I felt a little strange about it," Marta says shyly. "To be honest, I never had any experience like that before, so I didn't know what it would be like to have this little person sucking on my breast almost twenty-four hours a day. The idea of being exposed to the world like that felt unnerving."

By the time her son was born, Marta was still on the fence about nursing. "I was almost wishing deep down that formula was better for babies," she admits. "Then, after the birth and when we were in the hospital and started trying to breastfeed, I had a total change in attitude. I was like, 'This isn't as weird as I thought it would be. This is a bonding thing.'" She left the hospital a new mother—and a committed breastfeeder.

As many babies do—nobody ever warns us about this, do they?—Marta's son had a difficult time latching on to her breast. After several unsuccessful attempts at teaching the pair different holds and latch tricks, a nurse at the hospital set Marta up with a nipple shield, a nipple-shaped silicone device designed to protect the nipple and help babies latch correctly. The little plastic hat worked right away, and soon her son was nursing like a champ. The nurse warned Marta that she would have to wean her son off the shield or her milk supply could dwindle, but the baby had other ideas.

"I just couldn't wean him off of it," Marta says. "He would scream every time I tried, and I didn't have the backbone to put up with it. I was like, 'This seems to be working.' So I kept using the shield."

When Marta went for a postpartum checkup with her ob-gyn, she agreed to get a shot of Depo-Provera. It seemed like an effortless method of birth control, and even though her doctor mentioned that there was a slight chance her milk supply could be adversely affected by the drug, Marta didn't really worry about it. Just a few weeks into new motherhood, she felt like her life was settling into a comfortable order. Maybe she'd be good at this mommy thing after all.

Then Marta took the baby in for his two-month checkup. When the pediatrician announced in a concerned tone that the baby had lost too much weight since his last visit, Marta felt like the rug had been pulled out from underneath her. When the doctor said Marta would have to take immediate action to keep her child healthy, Marta felt like a failure.

"I felt like a horrible mom," she confesses in a hushed, tearful tone. "He'd been unhealthy and losing weight all this time and I never knew it. I was thinking that we were doing great, but he was starving. How could I not have noticed that something was wrong?

"I don't know anything about babies," Marta continues. "I never babysat and I didn't have any brothers or sisters. I felt just horrible and guilty that he'd lost weight. My pediatrician sent me to a lactation consultant that day."

It turns out that Marta's breast milk had all but dried up. The baby was losing weight because he wasn't getting enough to eat. At their very first meeting, the lactation consultant helped Marta devise a program to get her milk supply up to speed. It was a complicated regime that included pumping as many as six times a day, taking the herbal supplement fenugreek and one prescription medicine, and feeding the baby formula at the breast with a supplemental nursing system (SNS).

"Every time he wanted to nurse, I had to make a bottle, connect it to the supplementer, and then tape these tubes to my breasts," Marta says, explaining that the tubes carry the formula to the baby, who feeds at the nipple, allowing for natural breast stimulation. "Then I needed to pump after each nursing, too, so I'd put him down and I'd pump as much as I could."

Day by day, Marta's supply began to increase. After a month of "pump, pump, pump—plus nine pills a day," her milk supply increased enough that she was able to feed the baby without the SNS. (Along the way, he'd let go of his nipple shield addiction.) By this time, her son was sleeping through the night, but Marta still set her alarm to get up and pump. "I didn't want to jinx it," she says. "By now, I was totally committed to getting it right. I wasn't going to screw up again."

When she says she *screwed up*, Marta is referring to what she saw as a series of early parenting missteps, including the struggle weaning her boy off the nipple shield, the decision to get the Depo shot, and her inability to notice her son's dramatic weight loss.

"I'm tall and skinny, so I just figured he was taking after me," Marta sighs. "Believe me, I felt so guilty about him losing weight that

I was determined to make the breastfeeding work. I knew I'd do anything to make it right. I just had to make up for it."

Dr. Swigart, for one, believes that Marta's brand of motherguilt is an unfortunate by-product of our dog-eat-dog Western society. "We live in a competitive world. Women are trained from an early age to be competitive with one another," she says. "When it comes to mothering, things get out of hand. First, there's the way you give birth—do you do a natural, drug-free labor? Or do you have lots of drugs or—god forbid—a Cesarean? And once the baby's born, there's the Apgar scale, and the kind of diapers you use, and whether or not you're going to go back to work again—and then to top it all off, there's breastfeeding, which comes with its own set of assumptions and load of guilt."

In the face of this pressure, sometimes women don't support one another. "Instead, we find ways to cut each other down," says Beth. "It sucks."

Marta definitely felt the sting of criticism. She'd spent enough time beating herself up for not noticing her son's weight loss. And she'd spent even more time trying to make up for the mistake. She didn't want anyone else to tell her that she wasn't being a good enough mother.

One day, Marta took her nursling to visit her friends at the bookshop where she'd worked part-time before his birth. She was reaching the end of her breastfeeding ordeal, using the SNS only occasionally and giving the baby a bottle of expressed breast milk once or twice a day. "I was talking to a bunch of people when my son got hungry and fussy," she recalls. "So I took out the bottle I had with me. One of the women said to me, 'Oh, you should be breastfeeding.'

"My first reaction was defensive, 'But this *is* breast milk! I express.' I felt I had to redeem myself, to explain what I was doing. Then I was angry—after all I was going through—pumping, tubes taped to my breasts, money spent, pills taken—and she was going to lecture me about breastfeeding? Then I realized that if I *were* formulafeeding, and my son was nearing four months old, what good would lectures about breastfeeding do?"

The experience—and her own reaction to it—made Marta take her own silent pledge that from here on out, she'd never judge another mother's actions before she knew the whole story. That's what she hopes other people will do for her, too.

"I don't make judgments about women and bottles anymore," she says firmly. "Mothering is hard enough."

Well put, Marta.

If we could all be a little easier on ourselves—and on other mothers—our lives would be so much better. If we could just dump all the stinky mamaguilt and celebrate our own little successes (She stopped biting! He slept through the night!), think of how much time we'd have left over for the really important stuff, like reading a good book or taking a walk or laughing with a friend. Of course, as mothers (or as women, for that matter), we'll never be totally free from guilt or worry—that's not the point here—but how about trying for a little less?

If everything about raising your baby worked exactly the way some books tell you it's supposed to, you wouldn't have very interesting stories to tell your girlfriends, would you? A perfect life may be guilt-free, but it's also boring. Imperfections are what make us interesting. I'd rather be *interesting* than *boring* any day.

The Mama Advisory Board on Mamaguilt

- **Don't judge—lest you be judged.** Barbara used to assume that all bottlefeeding mothers chose not to breastfeed. "Once I learned that I could nurse from only one breast, I stopped being so judgmental," she says. "Now I just assume that every mother is doing the best that she can."
- **Don't let anyone tell you that breastfeeding is *always* wonderful.** "It took me three months before I enjoyed it," Allison says. "No one ever told me that it could take that long."
- If you're ever worried that your baby isn't getting enough to eat, **take him to the doctor's office and get him weighed,** Marta says: "Since you can't measure the amount of breast milk he's getting, weighing your baby will be the best way to know if he's growing at a healthy rate. No pediatrician should ever make you feel bad for doing that."
- **Don't let someone else guilt you into weaning.** Liz believes that the decision to wind down breastfeeding should be made by you and your kid—and no one else: "Only you know what's best for your child. What other people think really shouldn't carry all that much weight."

Chapter 3

Love-In

Letdown orgasms, baby bonding, and the joy of it all

I f you cracked this book open and, like a good girl—though I'm betting that you, dear reader, don't like to think of yourself as a *good girl*—read straight through from the introduction to chapters 1, 2, and so forth, you may be wondering why I waited until chapter 3 to jump into the happy bath of breastfeeding stories, the blissed-out tales of glowing, cherub-faced babies and the earth mothers who suckle them.

Let me put it this way: Learning to breastfeed is a little like learning to ride a bike.

One warm spring morning not that long ago, I watched as my then-six-year-old neighbor, smart, spunky Elly, set out to learn how to ride her two-wheeler. After her father obligingly removed the training wheels she'd been relying on for years, Elly strapped on her helmet and knee pads and bravely claimed a patch of sidewalk. My then-three-year-old was busy scooting around on her trike, and so from my perch on our front stoop, I witnessed Elly's maiden voyage.

At first, Elly tried the traditional method, with her dad running along beside the bike and then letting her go, only to watch her wobble for a few anxious seconds and then crash to the concrete with a disappointing thud. With a brave, determined set to her jaw, Elly tried it this way several more times, each fall a heartaching

47

disappointment—she had thought it would be so easy! Eventually, with a tearful wave of her hand, she told her father to go away. The sun continued to rise, and as Elly sat sniffling on the grassy boulevard, I imagined that she was considering whether a twelve-year-old would get teased for using training wheels. But after a moment's reflection, Elly reset her shoulders and shook her hair out of her eyes. Then she picked up the bike and set out to teach herself how to ride.

There were more crashes and many more tears, but by the end of that long day, Elly had mastered the art of the bike. As the sun began to set on our quiet dead-end street, she could be seen zipping up and down the sidewalk on her two-wheeled steed, leaving an awestruck gaggle of littler kids in her dust.

Later, when the time came for Elly's younger sister to remove her training wheels, having an experienced older sibling there to help her through the rough patches made the transition to big-girl bike that much easier. The two now rule the neighborhood: For these sassy sisters, hopping on their bikes and racing up and down in front of the house is easier than walking.

Many months later, I asked Elly to recount her memories of this great day, and it was difficult for her to recall that learning to ride her bike was ever hard to begin with. But it *was* hard, which made her success—the moment when Elly realized that she was gliding along alone, not wobbling or crashing but fast and free—all that much more exhilarating.

In many respects, it's the same with breastfeeding. There can be a lot of crashes on the way to becoming a successful breastfeeder, but there is also an immense feeling of satisfaction that comes once the skill is mastered. Breastfeeding is a thrilling, empowering accomplishment, to be sure, and once you've got it down—and I swear I'm not lying to you when I say that most mothers and babies do eventually figure it out—nursing your child can feel like an act of pure love, a psychic connection that will never be severed. On a practical level, it's also pretty damn cool. Your baby is hungry or tired or stressed out, and you have what she needs, conveniently packaged and ready for consumption right there on your chest. This realization may be enough to make all the work feel worthwhile, and, like Elly, you may even forget that it was ever hard in the first place.

Nurser's High

Kara, a thirty-five-year-old special education teacher from Norco, California, struggled with her "supremely attached" newborn, a healthy but sensitive baby who nursed practically nonstop for the first four months of her life. Not one to mince words, Kara explains the situation like this: "Basically, if I had my shirt open, she'd be there sucking on me. If I didn't have my shirt open, she'd be crying and whining for me to let her at 'em."

This overwhelming need to nurse is common among newborns, says lactation consultant Catherine Adeboye, RN, IBCLC from St. Paul, Minnesota. "There's more to breastfeeding than the milk," she explains. "In this culture, we like to think of nursing as a means to deliver food, but for the baby, it's so much more. In the days following birth, a baby doesn't yet realize that he or she is a separate individual. It's not that the baby really needs to eat that much; it's just that they have been thrust into the world with no warning and they need to reconnect to their mother, to understand that she is still there even though she suddenly seems very far away."

Fully aware of her daughter's needs for continued connection, Kara structured her life around those needs for the first few months of her existence, nursing on demand and providing constant contact and comfort. Most of the time, Kara was happy for the extra hours with her precious newborn, but there were also days when it felt like a tough slog, and she felt relieved when her little girl slowly began to realize that there was a world beyond her mother's breasts.

With a bit of patience and some gentle encouragement ("I put her in the Baby Bjorn facing out, so she could see other things besides my chest," Kara laughs), the baby adapted to what felt like a more manageable schedule of regular feedings with two- to three-hour breaks between. Slowly, mother and child slipped into a comfortable routine.

Kara says that breastfeeding has now become easy, "like brushing my teeth or combing my hair. It's just part of what I do during the day." But, she adds, she hasn't forgotten that nursing didn't always feel easy *or* natural. When things got tough with her daughter, Kara was helped along by memories of nursing her first child, a now-five-year-old boy. Her son was premature, Kara explains, and their breastfeeding relationship got off to a rocky start. Still, Kara stuck with it, pumping and storing enough milk to feed her son for his first year—even when she underwent surgery for cervical cancer.

"I got a little bit obsessed about storing my milk," Kara recalls, "but when I went in for surgery, I was able to say to my husband, 'In case something bad happens to me, just open the freezer. You'll be thankful.'"

Now five years cancer-free, Kara was overjoyed when she was able to conceive and give birth to her daughter. Because of everything that she's gone through, Kara says that breastfeeding now carries special significance. And now that she's gotten over the hardest part, nursing feels almost like a sacred duty, an honor.

"You just have to have that stick-with-it mindset," Kara says. "It's like when you go running and at first you think you're going to pass out, but you push yourself through that, hit a wall, and then suddenly you're at the point where you're running along and it feels good. You get that runner's high. I think there's a nurser's high, too. You've just got to push through the tough stuff to get to it."

It's Raining Hormones

If you've done any research on breastfeeding, you've probably read that for many mothers, nursing feels good. Not just plain good, like "I'm doing a healthy thing for my baby. Isn't that nice?" but *gooood*, as in *sensual pleasure* good.

For a small number of nursing mothers, the act of breastfeeding—after the initial awkward stages—brings on physical sensations that are similar to those experienced during sexual arousal. For another, larger group, breastfeeding stimulates powerful feelings of relaxation, deep calmness, and watchful love.

Blame it on the oxytocin. A hormone secreted during breastfeeding, oxytocin causes breast milk to be released into a mother's milk ducts, then into her milk sinuses, and eventually into her baby's mouth. Oxytocin is responsible for the tingling sensation, or "letdown," that most mothers experience as their milk begins to flow. It is also the hormone that stimulates uterine cramping associated with early breastfeeding, a sign that your uterus (and, hopefully, your belly) is shrinking back to something resembling its pre-pregnancy size.

The reason some women are aroused during breastfeeding may have to do with the fact that oxytocin is also the hormone that causes contractions during female orgasm. The connections between motherhood, birth, and sexuality start to get tangled up here, especially when you learn that labor contractions are also caused by oxytocin.

You don't have to go back all that far, only to the beginnings of the "natural birth" movement of the late 1960s or early 1970s, to hear women compare the feelings aroused by a healthy, unencumbered birth with those stirred by a good roll in the hay. Now don't let this freak you out—I'll talk at length about the sex/breasts/body/baby connection in chapter 6—for now just bear in mind that those pleasurable feelings may be a sign that God really *is* a woman, and all that oxytocin pumping through your veins is working its wacky, womanly magic on your mental, physical, and sexual health.

Over the last decade, more and more scientists have been focusing on oxytocin and its positive impact on women's health. For instance, Kathleen Light, PhD, professor of psychiatry at the University of North Carolina/Chapel Hill Medical School, linked increased oxytocin levels found in nursing mothers with lower blood pressure levels. And in a study conducted at UCLA, Laura Cousin Klein, PhD, now professor of behavioral health at Pennsylvania State University in University Park, connected oxytocin release with stress response in women, concluding that the hormone causes a "tend and befriend" impulse, encouraging the care of children and gathering with other women—rather than the more heavily studied (and now believed to be more innately male) "fight or flight" impulse.

"Oxytocin is the hormone of bonding. It has its physical functions, but it also has functions that affect psychological behavior," says Adeboye. "Some people aren't comfortable with the idea that bonding to an infant is not just an emotional act, it's also a chemical one. But I tell them that it is just nature's way of ensuring that we care for our young."

In the first days or weeks after giving birth, many women find themselves more vulnerable to powerful physical and emotional sensations than ever before. Their veins pump with a potent cocktail of hormones; they feel things deeply, tasting, smelling, and seeing the world with greater intensity. It's like PMS times ten, a mix of emotions that are both positive and negative.

I recall those first few days after my daughter was born as a wild ride between exhaustion, elation, confusion, pride, and fear. (Like the time my hospital-grade pump clogged with milk and inexplicably exploded, and I nearly collapsed on the floor in tears.) Later, once I figured out nursing, there were times when I looked at my little Bean with the most powerful love I'd ever felt, when my heart swelled and my toes curled with pleasure. But there were also times—mostly early on—when I wanted to peel that screaming little bundle off my sweaty chest, hand her over to the nearest capable adult, and run for my life.

It's those intense emotions—combined with deserved pride in the accomplishment of bringing a new person into the world—that inspire some women to wax poetic about the experience of motherhood. Add breastfeeding (and its tag-along pal oxytocin) to the mix, and you can't blame a mother if her loveometer goes off the charts. I'm no cornball, but even *I* experienced my share of oxytocin trips, quietly powerful moments of middle-of-the-night inspiration when I wanted to write sonnets about my daughter's feathery hands, her curving seashell ears, and her soft, silken cheeks.

I never actually *did* put a sonnet down on paper, but I wrote hundreds of them in my head. This is hard for a wizened old cynic like me to admit, but there were many moments when I'd look down at my beautiful nursing girl and think, "No mother has ever loved her child as much as I love you," or "You are the most beautiful creature who has ever lived." I might have chuckled at myself at the time, but I meant it, and I still do.

As those powerful surges of mamalove knocked me off my feet and turned me into a sniveling, joyful, lovesick puddle of emotions, I was reminded of how I felt when I first met my babydaddy (a.k.a. my husband). For months, I walked around in a state of heightened emotion, sleep deprived, bursting with love and revved up with sexual tension. Like the first few months of my daughter's life, the first few months of this all-consuming love affair was an exhausting time—but a time I wouldn't trade for anything in the world.

Worth It, but Wearing

No one can question whether Kathy is committed to breastfeeding. A firm believer in the principles of attachment parenting, the granola supermama from Olympia, Washington, decided from the start that she would nurse on her daughter's schedule until the little girl was ready to wean herself. Though she understood that getting started could be hard, Kathy fully expected that one day, breastfeeding would become something she looked forward to, an opportunity to spend restful time with her daughter as she grew from baby to toddler to child.

But as it turned out, breastfeeding has never been a piece of cake for Kathy. To begin with, her daughter had a particularly difficult time learning to latch, and Kathy, who had read all the definitive books on nursing and enlisted an army of lactation consultants, felt frustrated that she couldn't make what was supposed to be a natural act *feel* more natural. "It was really hard," she admits. "It took two whole months for us to get a latch that worked. Until we figured it out, my kid was miserable—and so was I. She was screaming all the time because she couldn't get enough to eat."

As a stopgap measure, Kathy pumped milk, and her husband fed the baby with an SNS tube taped to his finger. This system worked well enough for a few days—the infant was getting enough nutrition—but everyone in the family knew that things couldn't continue this way. Kathy and her daughter made several trips to the lactation consultant and attended local La Leche League meetings. Kathy also spoke with other nursing mothers and, she explains dryly, "just stuck her on me over and over and over again."

After witnessing mother and daughter struggle through a particularly difficult nursing session—or listening to Kathy complain of cracked nipples and thrush—well-meaning friends and relatives would occasionally offer advice. "A couple of people said to me, 'Maybe you just can't do this,'" Kathy recalls. "I felt so righteous and angry when they said that. I was going to do it, dammit! If I hadn't been so determined to prove them wrong, I probably would've quit." Kathy persisted and was eventually rewarded with a successful latch.

She still remembers the day everything fell into place: "My daughter was eight weeks old. One day, out of nowhere, she latched correctly. I looked down at her and I was like"—Kathy laughs a little sheepishly—"'I really *do* love this baby.'"

The long battle finally won, both mother and child settled into what they hoped would be a long, successful nursing relationship. Kathy's little girl, for her part, grew to be particularly fond of breastfeeding, turning to her mother for nutrition, comfort, and assurance countless times a day. But for Kathy, nursing wasn't always as easy or comfortable as she imagined it would be. Sure, there were plenty of times when mother and daughter made one of those special, oxytocin-fueled connections. ("She'd gaze up into my eyes. That was pretty sweet. And then it would feel relaxing. The hormones were kicking in.") But there were also moments when Kathy felt overwhelmed and overcrowded, when her sweet baby would whine, demand, and bite.

"Even though I was committed to being there for her," Kathy recalls, "I'd want to get away from her—even for just an hour or two. But I couldn't, really. We were attached at the boob."

Linda Blum, PhD, the professor of sociology at the University of New Hampshire in Durham and author of *At the Breast,* says that even the most committed, attached mother like Kathy can experience moments of self-doubt. And when the expectation (either self-created or culturally inflicted) is that a mother will carry the bulk of the responsibility for a child's health and well-being, the need to escape can become especially acute.

For middle-class mothers in 1950s and 1960s America, the cultural ideal was June Cleaver, the icon of American femininity and motherhood. Today, many liberal-minded parents look up to William and Martha Sears, authors of *The Baby Book,* the parenting bible for committed attachment parents like Kathy.

"Despite our gains over the decades, many mothers today still find themselves in the same frustrating situation," Dr. Blum says. "When my children were infants, I remember wondering, 'Why can't I just have one night a week where I go to a movie?' But in the first few months, your body doesn't always cooperate. I'd find myself at the movies saying, 'I can sit here and watch a movie in pain and risk getting a breast infection, or I can go to the woman's room and try to pump my breasts.' Neither felt like a good option. If your goal is to be as attached as possible, most times you'd likely think twice about going out alone at all."

When Kathy's baby was just six months old, Kathy's period started again. "Around this time, I started getting plugged ducts," she recalls, adding that she has always suspected that the new hormonal surge may have caused her breasts to start clogging up. "I kept getting them and getting them. It went on for months. It was bad. After all my early work and our seeming success, to experience difficulty like that again was really humbling—and depressing—for me."

But despite Kathy's obvious discomfort, her daughter showed no signs of giving up the breast. Kathy, true to her earlier commitments, kept at it for four years (the plugged duct problem eventually resolved itself). Then, when Kathy became pregnant again, her preschool-aged daughter finally threw in the towel. With only the slightest hesitation, Kathy admits that this break was a welcome relief.

"I need this time on my own," she explains. "I'm getting ready for another baby now, and I think my body needs some kind of small break before everything starts over again." Still, there are times when Kathy misses the special connection that grew out of her breastfeeding relationship. Even though it wasn't always the blissful time she anticipated, Kathy still has warm memories of the gift she gave her daughter—and she has hopes that nursing will be easier the second time around.

"I know this sounds strange, but I feel like I deserve more of those hormonal surges," Kathy laughs. "Maybe next time, things will work a little more smoothly. But from here on out, I'm focused on being realistic."

The Booby Prize

Kristin, the thirty-two-year-old account manager, always understood that breastfeeding offered health benefits for babies, but she had no idea that lactation could also work wonders for her social life.

"When I was six months postpartum, my sister got married," she says. "I was breastfeeding then, and"—gesturing at her chest with her hands—"I was *big*. I have never been a busty woman, never in my life. But at this wedding I had major cleavage. And I was showing it off—let me tell you. That night, every one of the groomsmen wanted to have his picture taken with me."

For Kristin, this temporary, silicone-free breast enlargement was just one in a long list of breastfeeding bennies, unexpected "booby prizes" that she discovered during the seventeen months she spent nursing her son.

After spending the first few weeks working out the kinks (her baby had jaundice and was sleepy, and Kristin's bounteous breasts had an embarrassing tendency to leak), the pair became a well-oiled mama-baby nursing machine. Even after her maternity leave was over and she'd returned to her full-time job, for Kristin, breastfeeding remained a sensual—and emotional—pleasure that she looked forward to every day. "I've never felt like my animal nature was as apparent as it was then," Kristin says. "I *felt* everything that much more strongly. It was like someone had turned up the volume on my body. I loved it."

Another positive side effect of breastfeeding was the way Kristin's baby weight just melted off. "I ate and ate and ate and ate and could not eat enough," she laughs. "I ate everything, especially dairy products. I couldn't get enough cheese. In truth, my body's ability to burn calories was a real impediment to weaning. I could literally eat anything I wanted to and I'd still lose weight."

Breastfeeding was also convenient. Because Kristin and her husband sleep in the same bed as their son, she says that after the first few months, she hardly even woke up when the baby needed to eat. "All I had to do when he was hungry was just roll over and lift up my shirt," Kristin says. "And when he got older, he would just pound on me when he wanted to eat. I would roll over, lift up my shirt, and that was that. It was so much more convenient than making a bottle."

I hate to admit this, but I used to stereotype hard-core lactivists. I assumed it was a motley army, this corps of committed breastfeeders. They sported a uniform of sorts: Guatemalan-print babyslings, shapeless German sandals, and pilly, baggy-kneed sweatpants. It was a group I admired, but, as far as I understood, it was a small group, one that existed only on the edges of society. Then I started looking around and realized that I was dead wrong. There are plenty of sling/sandal/sweatpants nursing mamas, but there are also plenty of minivan/Merrill/Motorola mommies, and even a few briefcase/Blahnik/bustier boobie babes, too. Understanding that just about any type of woman could be committed to breastfeeding rights meant that I could be, too.

An efficient, dedicated career woman, Kristin didn't fit my stereotype of a hard-core lactivist. But in many ways she is. The experience of breastfeeding turned out to be so positive for both Kristin and her son that when the topic is raised, she turns almost evangelical. Her husband shares her feelings. After a softball game one summer, he nearly got into a bar fight with a man who said he thought seeing a baby at the breast was gross. "He came home and told me about it, and I was so proud of him," Kristin recalls. "A man who defends breastfeeding is just sexy."

Occasionally, friends and coworkers will tell Kristin about their breastfeeding woes. There are times when she tries to keep her opinions to herself, but most of the time she can't resist the opportunity to climb up onto her soapbox.

"If it's very early on, I'll say, '*Do not* think about quitting before three weeks. You have to give it at least three weeks,'" Kristin explains to them. "I have friends who have stopped early, and I definitely think it was premature. It's such a shame. Both the mother and the baby are missing out on so much. Now if someone asks me for advice, I let them know my opinion right away. 'It gets easier,' I'll tell them. 'It takes a while for you to learn your baby and for your baby to learn you, but once you've got that down, it's a wonderful thing.' I'm always telling people, 'You might have to gut it out at first, but the payoff is incredible.'"

The Golden Moment

We're all out for one thing in this life. I'm not talking about unlimited money or sex or sudden fame. I'm talking about something much quieter but much, much larger—a sensation I'll call the Big Payoff, the golden moment when you are rewarded for all your hard work and tenacity with the sudden realization that everything is exactly as it's meant to be.

You might have a hard time believing this right now, but a mother's life is full of Big Payoffs, awestruck moments of wonder at the little human being who has innocently entrusted itself to your care. To begin with, there's birth, a scene that's been depicted in countless movies, sitcoms, and documentaries.

From *Nine Months* to *Friends* and *A Baby Story,* we've seen scripted labor and birth so many times that we expect the real thing to end the same way: a triumphant, softly glowing mother and a haggard-yet-proud father cradling a warm infant in their clean hospital bed. But even if your birth had absolutely no resemblance to the ones you've witnessed on the big (or little) screen, in all likelihood there was still that *moment* when you saw your child for the first time, when you touched his warm, slippery skin or looked into her clear, confused eyes. Even if up to this moment you were too cynical to believe in miracles, when your baby was born, the earth shifted beneath your feet and you witnessed firsthand the power of creation.

For an hour, maybe even five, the miracle of your child's birth feels like it will be enough payoff to last a lifetime, but because we are human, we soon start wanting more. Mothers who choose to breastfeed may anticipate the next Big Payoff to come right away, when the baby is placed on their breast, latches immediately, and begins the seamless transition from womb to world.

But that transition is rarely seamless. For most mothers and babies, there are a lot of small disappointments on the way to the Big Payoff. For me, the sting from those disappointments felt particularly sharp. I wanted a storybook ending, and I wanted it *now*. When the golden moment felt like a distant shadow on the horizon, time slowed to a crawl, and the weeks that it took to get breastfeeding to feel natural for me felt like months, even years.

Ayun Halliday, creator of the funky mamazine *East Village Inky* and author of the alternative parenting memoir *The Big Rumpus,* decided back when she was a teenager that when she had children of her own, she was going to breastfeed them. "I think a lot of my fantasy image of motherhood was developed when I was in high school," Halliday says. "I wanted to be a hippie and bake homemade bread and live in this house with a scarred old farmer's table. I imagined myself giving birth naturally in a field somewhere and breastfeeding my babies like an earth mother."

But Halliday's expectations for the perfect, natural hippiebirth were thrown out of whack when her daughter, India, came into the world after a long, harrowing labor that ended not (as intended) at the local birth center in a cloud of incense but rather at a nearby hospital in a stench of antiseptic. Shortly after India's birth, she

India developed a mysterious, life-threatening infection and had to be transferred to the NICU. Halliday, who had envisioned her birth story fading to black with a crunchy version of the "glowing-mother-proud-father" shot, instead was presented with a small, sickly infant encased in a clear-plastic isolette. For several days, the Big Payoff seemed illusive.

Despite the forced separation from her child, Halliday remained determined to breastfeed, and she pumped around the clock, delivering "little, tiny bottles" of colostrum to the nurses' station each night. She fought off depression by focusing on the future and on the connection she hoped to forge once India's health improved.

As it turned out, the Big Payoff came sooner than anyone expected. India was still in the NICU when Halliday, a notorious insomniac, decided to pay her a 4:00 A.M. visit. "One of the nurses said to me, 'Do you think you want to try to feed her?'" Halliday recalls. "To me, that was a sign that this nurse was saying India was going to be okay. I picked her up carefully, put her to my breast, and she latched on right away. I sat there in the NICU rocking chair and just *glowed*. I remember it as this euphoric triumph, this completely transcendent moment."

Soon, India was healthy enough to go home, and Halliday could finally create the kind of life she had dreamed about. Once things settled back to a normal routine, she realized that while she would never have the scarred kitchen table/homemade bread household of her childhood fantasy, she *could* breastfeed. Knowing that this was one thing that she could do—and do well—made up for her earlier disappointments. After her awkward start, Halliday realized that she enjoyed breastfeeding and that it was something she was good at, and that was enough to satisfy her for a long time to come.

"I have this picture that was taken of me breastfeeding India when she was a baby," Halliday recalls. "I don't know if I've ever been so happy. Here was this incredible moment of delayed gratification. I've never looked back again."

The Mama Advisory Board on Lactationlove

- **Having a supportive partner helps make breastfeeding even more pleasurable,** Kristin says. "If your husband's behind your decision to nurse, odds are you'll do it that much longer. Make sure he understands how important breast milk is for the health of your baby. Ask him to stand up for you if others object to what you're doing. Breastfeeding made me feel sexier. I made a point of letting him know that."

- Kathy's post-period plugged ducts were a real pain in the *breasts,* but she's decided to think of them as **nature's way of boosting her breast health** long-term. "When I was going through that, I got it in my mind that by getting rid of the plugs, I was flushing out my ducts," she says. "I feel like there was junk in my breasts that needed to get worked out, and now I feel like by breasts are better for it."

- **Don't forget about the nurser's high.** Remember Kara's comparison of it to the runner's high: "You've just got to push through the tough stuff to get to it."

Chapter 4

You Got a Problem with That?

Taking your breasts public

I
t was only midmorning, but Kitani the gorilla already looked exhausted, lying faceup on the hard dirt ground of her pen at the
Toledo Zoo. One large, rough hand was plastered on her fore-
head, and her eyes were clouded with fatigue. Oblivious to her
mother's condition, Nia Lewa, Kitani's hyperactive toddler, clam-
bered up and over her mother's body, first poking a finger in her eye,
then planting a dirty foot on her mouth.

Heaving what looked like the primate equivalent of a heavy sigh,
Kitani scooped up Nia Lewa and in one deft move latched her baby
to her exposed, surprisingly human-looking breast. Nia Lewa rooted
a minute, and then her body relaxed as she sprawled companionably
atop her mother, nursing intently. In the blink of an eye, she was
calm, quiet, and—best of all—fast asleep.

From my perch in the visitors' gallery, I watched this family
drama unfold. Admittedly, few human mothers are expected to nurse
in front of a herd of curious onlookers, but for some reason I felt a
strange sense of déjà vu. There are times—especially during the awkward early weeks—when the thought of breastfeeding an infant out
in the open can make even the most well-adjusted mother feel like
a monkey in a zoo. She may fear that if she chooses to exercise her

God-given right to whip 'em out in public, the eyes of the world will suddenly be focused on her lactating breasts, and everyone—from Grandma and Aunt Mabel to the paperboy—will be given license to comment.

My neck tensed involuntarily as I waited for one of my fellow zoo-goers to make a snide remark about the simian sideshow going on beneath our very noses. But no one seemed to notice. Or care—least of all Kitani. As she shifted under the weight of her sleeping infant, she closed her eyes contentedly. Peace at last. And so easy to achieve. For the first time in my life, I was jealous of a gorilla.

Now don't get me wrong: I'm not comparing *Homo sapiens* mothers with gorillas (though from what I read, some gorillas are just as advanced as many of *my* human relatives). And I'm not even advocating for breastfeeding Kitani-style: topless, sprawled flat on your back in the middle of the action. But what I am saying is that this particular gorilla's ability to unselfconsciously feed her infant, to satisfy both her child's needs *and* her own in less time than it takes a formulafeeding mother to screw a nipple on a bottle, felt emboldening.

I know I'm not the only mother in the world who ever got flustered at the idea of nursing her child in public. Before my kid was born, I never even thought about what I'd do if someday we were out somewhere and she needed to eat—*now*. Maybe I believed that the Booby Fairy would float down from the heavens and present us with a warm, sterilized bottle of fresh breast milk—who knows? But I'm the kind of person who likes to get out of the house, to see other adults and hold my face up to the bright morning sunshine. So it wasn't all that long before the inevitable happened.

When it did, I took a deep breath, gauged the mood of the room, and popped her on, bravely carrying on conversation and smiling as nonchalantly as possible. The next time it happened, I didn't need to take as deep of a breath. But still, nursing my daughter in public never felt like second nature to me—and in many ways, I wish it had. It would have made my life that much easier.

Portability ranks high among breastfeeding's many advantages.

Once a mama has established a healthy latch and a comfortable Boppy-free hold, her bare-bones diaper bag (or Duluth Pack or Kate Spade tote) need carry only diapers, wipes, and an extra set or two of baby clothes. From my own experience, lumpy bottles, nipples, and formula ruin the line of an ensemble. (Admittedly, so do massively engorged breasts and poochy, stretched-out tummies, but those are rightfully earned—and usually temporary—battle scars that can be carried off with pride).

Like any modern, emancipated woman, the words *freedom* and *independence* speak volumes to me. Although a mother's never completely free *or* independent again (a hard truth that slapped me in the face only minutes after my child was born), she *can* be freewheeling and indestructible if she's got breasts and she's willing to use them when the time is right. The key is getting past that all-too-present barrier of self-consciousness.

For many, comfort with public breastfeeding is a skill that comes with time. Kara, the mother of two from Norco, California, says that when her son was born, she felt uncharacteristically sensitive to the judgment of others. That meant she didn't always feel comfortable breastfeeding with other people around—even her family.

"I'll admit that there was a lot of covering up back then," Kara laughs. "Around my family, I definitely got the message that my breastfeeding presence wasn't all that welcome. If I was nursing in front of one of them, they would avert their gaze and suddenly come at me with a big towel or a blanket held out in front of their faces. Then they'd drape it over me and the baby. A lot of times, I would pump a bottle if I was going to my mom's house just to make everyone feel better. I didn't want to rock the boat."

Since the birth of her second child, Kara has become less willing to adjust her feeding schedule just to make other people feel comfortable. Somewhere along the line, she's also become far less self-conscious. Blame it on maturity, body confidence, or just good old-fashioned defiance—*Kara doesn't care anymore.* "Now I whip out my tit, and if they want to leave the room, they can," she says with a chuckle. "I've changed a lot. I figure I'm going to feed my kid where I want to feed her. If anybody has a problem with that, they can go blow."

Kara's newfound comfort with public breastfeeding extends not just to her family. California law protects the right of mothers to breastfeed their children in public, and Kara has chosen to exercise that right—even at the local mall.

One day she was out shopping with the baby and her daughter needed to eat. "She was getting ready to scream," Kara recalls. "It was a very conscious decision on my part to say, 'I am going to sit out in the coffee area, and I am going to pop my boob out in the mall, and if anyone has a problem with it, I am going to call all my mom friends and we are going to get together and nurse our babies right here.' In fact, the only thing that happened was that one little old lady came up to me and said, 'That's so beautiful, you feeding your baby like that.'"

Since she's taken her breasts public (so to speak), Kara has been surprised by the positive reactions she's received from strangers— and we're not just talking dirty old men or curious teenage boys. She admits that she often worries that people will object—and just like at the mall, she gears herself up for a fight—but so far nobody has raised an objection. She says she tries to be as discreet as possible when nursing, but she doesn't "go overboard," covering up with blankets, shawls, or burp cloths: "That just draws more attention to what I'm doing," Kara says, "like I'm wearing a sign that says, 'Nursing Mother over Here!'" Instead, she simply unbuttons her blouse (from the waist up, for better coverage), pulls her daughter in close, and carries on as if nothing out of the ordinary were happening. And, of course, nothing is.

"One time we were in this downtown plaza," Kara recalls. "I was sitting on this bench feeding the baby, when a man came by. He was obviously indigent. I got a little scared, like, 'This guy is going to do something.' He came by, took a look at us, and said, 'Look at the beautiful baby.' When he got closer and realized what was going on, he said, 'Oh, you're nursing her. I'm sorry. I'll come back.' Later he stopped by again and we chatted a little bit, and he told me how great he thought it was that I was nursing my daughter. It was like all my fears disappeared because he was so appropriate."

The willingness of mothers like Kara to casually nurse their babies in public is the first step toward making breastfeeding seem like an everyday activity, says Marsha Walker, RN, a lactation consultant who serves on the board of directors for the Massachusetts Breastfeeding Coalition. In her role as a lactation consultant, Walker has been advising clients for more than twenty-five years about ways to make nursing a child in public feel more like a natural act than an indecent exposure.

"When it comes to the natural function of a woman's breasts, the United States is an extremely modest nation," Walker says. "It's ironic when you think about the kinds of things that we wear on the beach or to the mall. But for a number of reasons, a great percentage of American mothers are deathly afraid even to be seen breast-feeding. In this country, we associate bottles with feeding babies. And that's a shame. Because feeding babies is what breasts are for."

I often wonder why the same guys who drool over Pamela Anderson's rock-hard *Baywatch* boobies lose their lunch at the sight of a pair of breasts doing what they were made to do. Any nursing mother who's been asked to leave a restaurant or coffee shop can attest to our culture's strange, strained obsession with this particular part of the female anatomy. Makes a gal wonder why bursting-at-the-seams silicone-enhanced stripper boobs are considered *hot*, when what they really look like (to any been-there-done-that mama's eyes) are painfully engorged nursing breasts.

Many Americans—unlike people who live in other parts of the world—have never even seen a baby being breastfed. It's a sorry truth that Walker blames in part on the mixed messages our society delivers about the female body, as well as something she and other breastfeeding advocates like to call the "formula industry," a powerful economic force that she says contributes to the belief that artificial milk is as good as—or even better than—the milk produced by mothers. From her perspective, that's just not true.

"If we never see babies being breastfed, it will never seem like a natural act, and we will continue to rely on formula, because it will seem easier, cleaner, and simply more acceptable," Walker says. If more women were willing to breastfeed out in the open—and if they were supported by their friends and loved ones—others would begin to realize that public nursing doesn't have to be the slightest bit *tit-illating*. And, Walker adds, if more people understood that fact, more American mothers would breastfeed.

"When women come to see me, I always make a point of showing them how breastfeeding can be done discreetly," Walker says. "It doesn't have to involve a lot of exposure." She talks to her clients about nursing clothing, shirts and dresses designed with convenient, concealed flaps for modest breastfeeding. She also gives them tips for making regular clothes work as well as nursing clothes.

Lactation consultant Catherine Adeboye from St. Paul, Minnesota, tells her clients to practice nursing in front of a mirror. "That way, if you're concerned about it, you can see the best ways to avoid too much exposure," she says. "And you can see that it's actually not hard to do at all."

Alexis Martin Neely, a family attorney and breastfeeding advocate from Los Angeles, says that community awareness of the advantages of breast milk—combined with a greater acceptance of public breastfeeding—may be the only way to encourage more women to nurse their children. Neely explains that while the majority of Americans tell pollsters that they believe mothers' work benefits society as a whole, fewer are willing to walk the walk, supporting initiatives that make moms' lives easier. From Neely's point of view, legislation that protects a woman's right to breastfeed anywhere anytime is a step in the right direction.

"It's a round circle," she says. "Public awareness of the benefits of breastfeeding as well as comfort with the sight of a breastfeeding mother are essential to raising the breastfeeding rates in this country. If women don't feel comfortable nursing in public, if they feel they have to shut themselves away in order to nurse, they will quit early—or they won't breastfeed at all."

Over the years, Neely has provided legal advice and assistance to women who have been asked to stop breastfeeding in public places. One client of Neely's, a California mother, was volunteering at her older child's elementary school, when her younger child became hungry. She found a bench just outside the classroom and proceeded to nurse her infant. The school principal asked the mother to stop nursing or to move to an empty classroom or a bathroom. Neely represented the mother on a pro bono basis, and eventually they convinced the school board to adopt a resolution saying that mothers could breastfeed their infants on school grounds—as long as the child did not cause a disruption.

"While that resolution wasn't perfect, it was an acknowledgment that breastfeeding is not obscene, that it is an important part of mothering," Neely says. "The fact that any resistance remains on this issue never ceases to amaze me. I see it as a proxy for the way women and women's issues are viewed in our society."

Nationwide, some twenty-nine states currently have legislation protecting a mother's right to breastfeed in public; some state laws are more comprehensive than others. And breastfeeding legislation is pending in as many as three more states. On a national level, courts have found that breastfeeding is a Constitutionally protected right, a fact that many advocates, including Walker, like to emphasize.

"Women are strong," Walker says. "If we empower them with the knowledge that the law is on their side, many will go ahead and take that risk. Women have to learn not to skulk away if someone objects to public breastfeeding. They have to learn to say, 'It's my right. It's the law.' It's hard because you're so embarrassed, you're just mortified. But it's our right and we need to claim it."

New national legislation is also in the pipeline. In 2001, the Right to Breastfeed Act, introduced by New York Democratic Congresswoman Carolyn Maloney, was passed as part of the fiscal year 2001 budget. The act ensures a woman's right to breastfeed her child on any portion of federal property where the woman and her child are otherwise authorized to be. In 2002, Representative Maloney was able to include in the Special Supplemental Nutrition Program for

Women, Infants, and Children (WIC) reauthorization bill a measure that allows state agencies to use the WIC food program funds to provide educational materials on breastfeeding. It also allows state agencies to use additional WIC funds to purchase breast pumps. In 2003, Maloney also introduced the Breastfeeding Promotion Act, a law that proposes to extend the Civil Rights Act of 1964 to protect the rights of nursing mothers, provide tax incentives for businesses that provide lactation areas, require minimum safety standards for breast pumps, and make breastfeeding equipment tax-deductible for families.

The fact that lawmakers are beginning to recognize breastfeeding as a civil right is welcome news to Ayun Halliday, author of the alternative parenting memoir *The Big Rumpus*. Not one to stay cooped up at home, the mother of two breastfed her children on the road whenever—and wherever—the need arose. And because Halliday has never been a particularly modest person (she was a drama major in college), she never had to get over the "Ohmigod! I'm nursing in public!" hurdle that so many women face.

"Strange as it sounds, breastfeeding remains a political act in this country," Halliday says. "There's still too much shame and reluctance around it, so I think actually doing it—and doing it proudly—is a feminist act. I believe a child needing to be fed in a public space is completely within the bounds of good taste and necessity. No one has a right to object to that."

The idea that public breastfeeding—even *discreet* public breastfeeding—is a revolutionary act served as inspiration every time I fed my baby out in the open. As my nursling and I settled down on a secluded museum bench or in a tucked-away restaurant booth, I imagined I heard "I Am Woman (Hear Me Roar)" playing softly in the background. I told myself, "This is my right, dammit," and I held my head high, daring anyone to cross me. But the truth is, I don't think anyone even realized what was going on.

It wasn't all that long ago that Halliday's toddler son weaned himself, but even though her nursing days are now over, she's still committed to supporting other mothers through their own breastfeeding journeys. If that takes dismantling the taboos that surround our views of women's bodies, then she'll be there at the front of the line, swinging a sledgehammer. "What is it about our culture that makes women feel so shy about their bodies that they feel they can't just sit and breastfeed, even around their good friends or their families?" Halliday asks. "Clearly it's something about breasts and the way we think about them. I mean: If women elbowfed their babies, they'd do *that* anywhere without even blinking an eye."

But Halliday knows it will take more than the protests of a loud-mouthed broad from New York to convince ordinary Americans of the importance of supporting nursing mothers and their children. Like all breastfeeding advocates, she can quickly tick off a list of the benefits of breast milk, but she also realizes that not everyone has even heard about those benefits. Perhaps support for the cause needs to come from a higher power.

"Wouldn't it flip your wig if the First Lady came out someday and said, 'I'm going to be the *breastfeeding* First Lady, not the *literacy* First Lady?'" Halliday muses. "Then maybe things would really start changing all the way down the food chain."

Slow Down, Sister!

Before you start hatching plans for a citywide nurse-in, it's important to remember that despite lactivists' best efforts, public nursing is still not for everyone. This is America, where breasts are still *breasts,* and whether they're nobly employed or not, someone somewhere is still likely to get bent out of shape at the sight of naked, nursing boobies on the city bus or at the local grocery store. Just think about the ruckus that was raised by Janet "Nasty" Jackson's now-infamous Super Bowl "wardrobe malfunction." One three-second flash of nipple was enough to keep commentators talking for *weeks.*

In a way, you can't blame a person for doing a double take at the sight of a nursing mother and child. Our community standards of decency allow for women's breasts to be viewed in one way— and one way only. Linda Blum, PhD, the professor of sociology at the

University of New Hampshire in Durham and author of *At the Breast,* believes that the reason for much of the uneasiness surrounding public breastfeeding may be the fact that in Western culture, women's breasts are sexual objects only.

Making any connection between motherhood and sex is a cultural taboo. Because we humans have evolved beyond our gorilla ancestors, we need to hold ourselves to a higher standard of behavior, this belief holds. Breastfeeding may be considered acceptable—even laudable—but only when it is done in private, away from the eyes of strangers and impressionable children. If we breastfeed shamelessly, in clear view, we are in danger of ending up back in the jungle, back where we started.

"In American culture, girls learn from an early age that the focus is on our breasts," Dr. Blum says. "When we make the choice to breastfeed, we're sending a message that we are choosing to use these objects that have been given so much sexual meaning for something other than sex, for their intended purpose. For many people, the connections get so close that it starts to get disturbing."

The differences in cultural attitudes about breastfeeding become particularly obvious when you've been away from this country for a few years. Becca, a twenty-eight-year-old systems analyst and mother of one, is an American citizen who met the man who eventually became her husband when she was studying in Chile. The couple married and settled there, living in the country until their son was a little over a year old. When she moved back to the United States and settled in Boston, Becca experienced the inevitable culture shock, but one of the things that surprised her the most about her home country was how unusual it was to see mothers breastfeeding their babies in public.

"Because Chile is a Latin American country that tends to be more outwardly conservative than the United States, I expected public breastfeeding to be more acceptable here than it was there," Becca says. "But that hasn't been the case at all. Not that anyone here has made negative comments or anything, but you just see more babies being nursed out in the open in Chile. There, you see more women and their children all the time, and public breast-feeding isn't a big deal. Here, I feel like I'm the only person doing it, and it freaks people out."

Public nursing's most vocal detractors include conservative social critics like Betsy Hart, whose weekly column is syndicated nationwide by the Scripps Howard news service. After observing a breastfeeding mother at a local gymnastics center "with her shirt just about up to her neck and with no discernable undergarments . . . feeding her not-so-young child, probably about fourteen months old," Hart, mother of four, was inspired to write a column for *The National Review.* Titled: "Take Cover! We're Seeing Way Too Many Breasts," the piece challenges what she sees as a trend toward broad acceptance of public breastfeeding.

"We've all heard that 'breast is best' when it comes to feeding infants," Hart wrote, adding that she breastfed her own children when they were young. "But does the entire village have to share in the process?"

Hart's argument is this: While breastfeeding is good for mothers and infants, public overexposure of breasts is not good for society. Just as a mother has the right to breastfeed her child, the public also has a right not to see her breasts. Therefore, Hart argues, legislation that supports a mother's right to breastfeed in public brings government into what is basically an issue of common decency: It's typical liberal tinkering with morality, and by shaping public breastfeeding into a civil rights issue, lactivists are forcing their moral choices on others.

"Breastfeeding advocates are actively pushing legislation in about thirty states that would enforce 'breastfeeding anywhere anytime' laws," Hart wrote. "Many states, like California—no surprise—already have such legislation. And throughout the country, lawsuits over the public breastfeeding issue are rife. Guess who almost always wins?"

But not everyone who's uncomfortable with the concept of

PDB—or Public Display of Breasts—has a political agenda. Many are just regular moms like Amy, a thirty-three-year-old mother of two and an online editor at a Midwestern daily. Amy's discomfort with the sight of a breastfeeding mother has nothing to do with politics—and everything to do with her own personal feelings about public nudity.

"With both of my kids, I would occasionally breastfeed in public," Amy explains, "but I'd always cover up. I have a friend who doesn't cover up at all when she nurses. For some reason, it makes me a little queasy."

Becca says that since she's moved back, she's noticed that same sort of reaction from some of her North American friends. "It's always a little bit embarrassing when I'm breastfeeding around people these days, because my son will start to nurse and then he'll get up and do something else, and I somehow end up with my breast just hanging out there," she says. "When that happens, even my female friends seem uncomfortable. I suppose they just don't see it that much, so they don't know what to expect."

With her first child, it took Amy a few months to work up the courage to nurse even in front of her friends. "It was a lot more isolating," she admits. "I remember being at a party not long after my first one was born, and I felt like I had to go into a private room while everyone else was outside. It was like, '*Whoo*. This is fun.' With my second, I felt more comfortable sitting on the deck and nursing around my friends, though I'm still not crazy about doing it around anyone else."

Jackie, the twenty-five-year-old community college instructor from Baltimore, Maryland, says the yogalike maneuvering that it took to get her twins latched at once made the idea of nursing them around strangers feel more like a chore than a time-saver. "I breastfed in public when I had to," she says. "I did it in a doctor's waiting room once. I did it in a mall a couple of times—but only because it was one of those days where if I didn't get out of the house I'd go crazy."

Because she literally didn't have a free hand when she was

nursing both of her daughters, Jackie says she felt particularly vulnerable breastfeeding them in a place where the sight of two babies
nursing at once might draw unwanted attention. She usually asked
her mom to come along on those out-of-the-house excursions, to
help set up the stroller, lift the car seats, and serve as a human shield
between the babies, her breasts, and the rest of the world.

"I'd find a hidden bench somewhere, block myself with a
stroller, and cover the babies' heads with a shirt flap," Jackie recalls.
"I went out of my way to be inconspicuous. One time I was in a mall,
and this woman had a couple of kids with her. She came up to us.
She was being really nice and she says something like, 'I think that's
so amazing.' I know she had the best intentions, but I felt conspic-
uous. I wanted to say something like, 'I'm trying to hide here. Don't
draw too much attention.'"

Jackie's discomfort with public breastfeeding may have played a
role in her decision to stop nursing her daughters when they were
seven months old. She's a woman who likes to get out of the house,
and she felt tied down by her own need to make feeding her babies
a (mostly) private event. Once her family introduced formula, Jackie
realized that she didn't always have to be the one responsible for
feeding. And because for Jackie, pulling out two *bottles* wasn't
charged with the same meaning as pulling out two *breasts,* bottlefeeding felt easier.

Lactation consultant and activist Marsha Walker says Jackie's
story illustrates her point: "If you're going to keep up exclusive
breastfeeding for any length of time, you've got to be willing to nurse
in public. If breastfeeding makes a woman feel limited in any way,
she's going to stop sooner rather than later."

That may be the case for Jackie, but in the end she felt satisfied
with her decision to stop. "You read in the books about mothers who
call breastfeeding an art, and you hear them talking about how beautiful it is," she says. "I definitely think it was the right thing for me
to do for my daughters when they were young, but I did not ever feel
those rushes of pleasure that everybody talks about. I wish I had. So

much of the time it felt complicated and cumbersome. Once we all stopped, I definitely felt better. I felt like myself again."

Amanda, a thrty-three-year-old marketing director from St. Paul, Minnesota, is the mother of three boys, one singleton and a set of twins. After working through the usual start-up problems, she successfully breastfed her oldest son until he was two and a half. Now she is perfectly comfortable breastfeeding her twins in public—she has even nursed them in her "totally nontraditional" workplace, during private meetings with her male boss—but she says it took time to get over the public exposure hurdle after her oldest child was born.

"The first time I saw somebody nurse, I was horrified," Amanda laughs. "I was in high school, and I was completely mortified that they would do that in public! I couldn't look! With my oldest son, at first I locked myself in the bedroom to nurse. But then my mother-in-law was visiting, and she knocked on the bedroom door and said, 'You need to talk to us while you nurse. You're not doing anything to be ashamed of.' That's when I realized that it was okay. From there on, more or less I've always been comfortable nursing in public, and if anyone asks me to go and do it somewhere else, I get offended. I'll say, 'I would never nurse my children in the bathroom. Would *you* ever eat in the bathroom?'"

Even though Amanda realizes that not everybody is comfortable with the sight of a breastfeeding mother—her younger self definitely wasn't, remember?—there's part of her that believes that the more commonplace public nursing becomes, the more natural it will seem. Amanda's willing to put herself—and her breasts—out there to make that point.

"I'll nurse my babies in public anywhere without a blanket or anything," Amanda says, defiantly. "Just the other day, I was at the mall. I was in plain view of everybody, but I just sat down and nursed them. My girlfriend was with me, and she said she saw an eighteen-year-old girl glance at me with this horrified look on her face. I think she even covered her eyes. It's pretty ironic, because that's what I was like back when I was her age, and now here I am, rocking her world."

Don't Rock the Boat, Baby

In some communities, the decision to breastfeed in public is simply a matter of personal choice, an act of mothering that many view as admirable, or at least inoffensive. In others, the sight of a breastfed baby is so rare that if a mother chooses to latch her infant on in public, she's likely to elicit negative comments or just simply feel unwelcome.

At least that's the perspective of Sharis, a 34-year-old stay-at-home mom and part-time editor of the blog RedHeadDred. Sharis, who is black, lives in Harlem, New York City's historic African American neighborhood. She nurses her daughter, a decision that makes her feel "proud, strong, and happy." But despite her conviction that breast is best, Sharis still doesn't feel particularly comfortable nursing her daughter when she's out running errands in her neighborhood. She said she hates being a target for nasty looks and negative comments. "In the black community," Sharis sighs, "people basically don't breastfeed. Even if you can't afford formula, breast milk isn't really considered an option by most people around here. I'm definitely outside of the norm."

It takes a lot of gumption to flaunt your decision to differ from community norms, especially around topics as charged as nursing and childrearing. It's one thing to flaunt your status as an outlier in a community far away from the one you call home, but in your own neighborhood, in the park across the street, or among the people you see every day, the rewards for fitting in are particularly high.

"When it comes to being a mother, there's definitely a lot of social pressure to do what everybody else is doing," says Mary Johnson, breastfeeding coordinator for the Minnesota WIC program. "If you don't, you better be ready to have your actions scrutinized pretty carefully."

Nationwide, African American mothers breastfeed at lower rates than do other ethnic groups. According to the 2003 Ross Mothers Survey, a survey conducted annually since 1955 by Abbot Laboratories, black mothers still lag behind their white and Hispanic counterparts when it comes to nursing, especially past the baby's first six months of life. Urban, majority-black communities like Harlem have some of the lowest breastfeeding rates in the nation, so Sharis's decision to nurse her daughter—and occasionally to do so in public—means that, in this respect at least, she has placed herself firmly outside of her peers.

Sharis has two much younger sisters, and her mother breastfed them, a decision that was considered unusual in her community even when they were babies. Watching her mother breastfeed her siblings—and listening to her reasons for making that decision—influenced Sharis to do the same when her daughter was born.

"I remember my mom talking about why she was going to breastfeed them," Sharis recalls. "She'd say, 'Cows' milk is for baby cows, and formula is soybeans. Why should you take something that's not designed for your body and give it to your child?' Even though I breastfeed my daughter, my mom was much more hard-core about breastfeeding rights. She and my husband see eye to eye on that. When it comes to breastfeeding in public and getting rude reactions, they have the attitude, 'Forget them.' Some days I'm up for the fight, and some days I'm not."

Sharis especially isn't interested in rocking the boat around members of her extended family. She says that she believes disapproval for breastfeeding is universal in much of the African American community, especially among older, rural folks.

"I was at a wedding down South," Sharis explains. "It was my grandmother's brother getting married, and so it was full of that generation of people. I just assumed they would have a problem with me feeding the baby in front of them. Also, I couldn't find a nursing dress, so I knew it would mean me getting half naked in front of a bunch of older folks, and I just couldn't do it. So I went into the bathroom, and an older woman at the wedding came in and saw what I was doing. She smiled and said, 'That is going to be one healthy baby.' I was all tensed up for a confrontation, but when she said that, I was so relieved. I thought Thank you for making my day."

On the other hand, Ola, the artist from Washington Heights, says she "defiantly" breastfeeds her daughter all over her neighborhood. Maybe it's because her neighborhood is home to more Latin American immigrants, but Ola says she feels comfortable nursing just about anywhere. On the rare times that someone objects to her PDB, she has a prepared response.

"Sometimes when I feed my daughter in the park, people stare, but *whatever*," Ola says. "Once or twice I've had little kids come up to me at the park and say, 'What are you doing? That's nasty.' I tell them. 'It's not nasty. I'm feeding her. I have milk with vitamins and nutrients in my breasts that keep my baby healthy and strong.'"

Although Ola's response to criticism shows an admirable level of conviction, Sharis's "don't rock the boat" reaction is far more commonplace.

"The whole issue of vulnerability—even for privileged mothers—is a reality all the time," Dr. Blum explains. "We continue to hear all of these stories about women being hassled for nursing in public. So mothers constantly have to gauge their comfort level before feeding their children. Add to the mix the idea of being a nonwhite person in a white society where your acceptability is constantly at risk anyway. What can make a woman in that situation decide that the benefits of breastfeeding outweigh the risks? Making the leap to do that requires real strength of character."

Sharis says that the level of acceptance of public breastfeeding varies depending on the neighborhood: "When I go to more-middle-class neighborhoods, the difference is phenomenal." "Of course, you can go sit on a park bench and feed your child there. But at home, you can't do that without getting a lot of looks. I'm usually pretty out there, but in my neighborhood, I am distinctly uncomfortable feeding my daughter in public, and even was when she was a newborn. My husband's like, 'Do what you want to do.' I'm like, 'I'm going to pay for this later.' I'm held to a completely different standard uptown."

The Ross survey claims that breastfeeding rates are at an all-time high in the United States, and that increases have been seen in all ethnic and racial groups. And African Americans have shown some of the most-significant gains. Sharis is heartened by this news, and she keeps her eyes peeled for evidence that the numbers are playing out in her community.

"Just the other day, I saw a woman in my neighborhood wearing a nursing shirt," Sharis laughs. "I was like, 'Another breastfeeder!' Can I embarrass her and ask, 'How's it going? How old is your child? Can we be friends?' It's pretty ridiculous, but sometimes I feel that desperate. I'd be so happy to know I wasn't the only one out there."

For the last four years, Wendy, a forty-year-old medical researcher and mother of two, has been conducting her own informal survey of breastfeeding trends in Jamaica Plain, Massachusetts, the diverse, vibrant community just outside of Boston that she and her family call home.

"Around here, the types of people I tend to see breastfeeding in public are mostly white and they mostly appear to be well-to-do," Wendy says, laughing at her own pseudo-scientific study. "I have not observed any Latinos or Asians breastfeeding in public."

Wendy, who is Chinese American, says she's particularly interested in the breastfeeding habits of Asians and other minority groups. She knows she's not the only Asian woman in her neighborhood who breastfeeds her child, but on some days she feels like she's the only one willing to do it outside of her home.

"It's entirely possible that the people I see bottlefeeding in public are breastfeeding in private," Wendy says. "I don't know. I try not to judge." Still, she's so convinced of the benefits of breastfeeding—and of the value of encouraging other people to view it as a natural, everyday occurrence—that she's willing to put herself out there, to discreetly but boldly nurse in public so that others can learn from her example.

"A long time ago, I set my mind that I am going to do this in public," Wendy says. "I told myself, 'I'm going to check out the situation, and if I feel comfortable doing it, I will.'" Echoing Ayun Halliday's declaration of her brood's right to occupy public space, Wendy holds firm to her conviction that even in public, a breastfeeding baby is a much more pleasant sight than a crying one. "My gut reaction is to react to my infant's needs as quickly as possible," she says. "If that means breastfeeding in front of other people, so be it."

Revolution Mom-Style, Now!

In the years before my daughter was born, I had this recurring nightmare: A wild, child-free woman becomes a mother and suddenly she starts acting like one. The killer heels end up at the back of the closet, the protest signs gather dust, the funky vintage convertible gets traded in for a navy blue minivan, and her sex life withers up and blows away. As the responsibilities of motherhood begin to weigh on her shoulders and cloud her mind, the wild woman even starts buying embroidered sweat suits—and wearing them *out of the house.*

The heroine of my nightmare wasn't me, exactly—I never could carry off stilettos, I never owned a vintage convertible, and, kid or not, you'd have to kill me before I'd wear a sweat suit anywhere. But she was an accurate representation of my fear that if I let my biological impulse to reproduce get the better of me, my marginally sassy, independent-grrrl lifestyle would end up in the toilet.

But then, as the desire to have a baby of my own morphed from an occasional inner whisper to an insistent whine, I started looking around at the mothers I knew. What I came to realize was that becoming a mother didn't necessarily have to make a gal close her eyes to the rest of the world or disappear under a pile of dirty diapers. In fact, what I learned was that the sudden realization of her inherent mamapower can actually inspire a woman to greater boldness than ever before.

Psychoanalyze my sweat suit phobia all you want, but you'll save yourself some time if you accept my theory that by lumping all practically dressed mothers into one plodding herd, I was doing the exact same thing that the rest of the world has been doing for eons: discounting the powerful potential of women with children. Since I started really *looking* at mothers—and talking to them about the minutia of their lives—I've begun to realize that whether we are

(continued on page 84)

How to Take a Stand

Legal experts answer common questions about breastfeeding rights

Until her death in 2003, Miami attorney Elizabeth N. Baldwin was considered the leading expert on breastfeeding legislation in the United States. As a member of La Leche League International's Legal Advisory Council, Baldwin provided legal council on hundreds of cases involving breastfeeding and attachment parenting. Because so many parents called Baldwin to request information about public breastfeeding laws, Baldwin, with the assistance of her husband, attorney Kenneth Friedman, prepared this helpful question-and-answer fact sheet for La Leche League's Web site.

Question: I am in a state with no breastfeeding legislation. Do I have the right to breastfeed in public?

Answer: Yes. The purpose of legislation is to clarify that it is legal, and to change society's attitudes about breastfeeding. As a general rule of thumb, if you have a right to be somewhere with your baby, and you can feed your baby a bottle, then certainly you have the right to breastfeed.

Question: I was asked to stop breastfeeding. What should I do?

Answer: If you are told to stop breastfeeding, you will have to decide whether you want to try to do something about it at the time, or to leave and take action later. If you decide to . . . do something about it at the time, you might ask if you can give your baby a bottle. If you are told that you can, you can . . . [let] them know that no one has the right to tell you how to feed your baby. If you are in a state that has legislation, let them know that there is a law that protects your right. If the establishment . . . [won't] bend, consider leaving and educating them later on.

If you are looking at how to handle it after the fact, look at the best way to educate those involved. If you are in a state with legislation, give them information about the laws, as well as about the importance of breastfeeding. If your state does not have any legislation, that does not mean you can't breastfeed! Consider using other states' legislation.

If you think you might want to take legal action against the establishment, consult with an attorney to determine your legal rights. Don't forget to visit the American Academy of Pediatrics' site and print out a copy of their recommendations (www.aap.org/policy/re9729.html). Nothing sets forth the importance of breastfeeding better than these recommendations!

Question: My state is considering enacting breastfeeding legislation. Is all breastfeeding legislation good, or are there certain types that should be avoided?

Answer: Not all breastfeeding legislation is positive. Any legislation that restricts or takes away the right to breastfeed should not be supported, and if it has already been enacted, steps should be taken to amend the statute taking out the restriction. For instance, Georgia and Missouri enacted laws trying to support breastfeeding mothers in public but put restrictions on it, requiring the mother to be discreet. . . . Yet, the purpose of legislation is to try to change these outdated views about breastfeeding and encourage more women to make this healthy choice. Thus, such language has a chilling effect on mothers, is not encouragement, and would authorize anyone who didn't think it was discreet enough to throw the mother out. This is why many of the states provided that a woman has a right to breastfeed even if there is exposure during or incidental to breastfeeding. Recognizing this, Georgia has submitted a bill that would delete this restrictive language. If your state is considering legislation, make sure no restrictions are included.

willing to admit it or not, we mamas are a pretty radical bunch. We love our children and we are willing to fight for them. We can still get passionate about what really matters, and when that passion is harnessed, we can make big changes in the world.

The recent cultural shift in attitudes about breastfeeding is a direct result of the passion of a group of mothers who managed to rouse themselves from the formula fog long enough to realize that breast milk is best for children and that everyone has a right to know the facts. The current preponderance of legislation supporting a woman's right to breastfeed in public enlarges the argument from a "mothers' issue" to a civil rights issue—a cause that speaks to a larger segment of the population.

You've probably heard about the Amazons, the mythical race of women warriors who cut off their right breasts to better shoot arrows at the enemies of women and children. Lately, I've been comparing nursing mothers with Amazons, thinking about the bravery (intentional or not) that's behind the impulse to bare one's own breasts—criticism or prying eyes be damned. Not every nursing mother thinks of herself as a bare-breasted Amazon, and not every brave mother breastfeeds, but the everyday stories of women like Kara and Jackie and Sharis and Ola reveal a deep conviction to do what's best for their children—even if it means risking the wrath of others.

That, as I like to say, takes ovaries. And that's what I'd call a *real* revolution.

The Mama Advisory Board on Baring Those Boobs

- **If you breastfeed discreetly, people rarely make a fuss,** says Kara. "Nobody's ever said anything negative to me. I think it's because I try to be really natural and relaxed about it. I don't make a big deal out of it, and I don't think most people can tell what's going on. It's pretty cool, actually."

- Worried about too much public exposure? Remember that lactation consultant Catherine Adeboye suggests you **nurse in front of a mirror** first. That way you can see what others will see. Then if you want to make some adjustments, you can.

- **Invest in some nursing clothes.** I especially like nursing tanks, stretch tops with a built-in bra and flaps that fold down from the top. This design provides tummy coverage, which for me, at least, felt key in those first flabby weeks after my babies were born. Once my tummy was covered, I felt like I could lift up my shirt and nurse just about anywhere.

- **Embrace your inner rebel.** "We have the *right* to nurse just about anywhere we damn well please," says Ayun Halliday. "Don't forget that. And don't ever let anyone tell you otherwise."

Chapter 5

Was My (Face) Red!

Sometimes, a gal can't do anything but laugh

Over the centuries, the image of a child at his mother's breast has been the subject of countless works of art. From Michelangelo to Rubens and Rivera, each artist's take on this universal theme is different, but they all depict a similar central image: a beatified mother and child, locked in an eternal embrace.

It's probably no coincidence that most of these artists are men. Anyone who's ever actually breastfed an infant—not to mention a toddler—knows that seven times out of ten, breastfeeding doesn't look anything like it does in paintings. Sure, every mama has her moments, times when nursing becomes the perfected image of love, ethereal enough to warm the heart and bring tears to the eyes. But real-life nursing also provides plenty of those other, more *earthy* moments, times when a baby is more chimp than cherub and a mother feels more madwoman than Madonna.

Still, it ain't all bad. Like I've said before, the sooner you accept the fact that being a mommy is an imperfect endeavor, the happier you'll be. Sure, a gal's gotta maintain her dignity, but all the breast-feeding veterans that I talked to assured me that their *absolutely most embarrassing* moments—the times when they were left with their breasts in the breeze and their cool composure in a puddle on the floor—eventually turned out to be some of the funniest moments in their lives. Get a couple of nursing mothers together, get them talking, and—like old Navy buddies telling war stories—before long they'll start topping each other with one outrageous breastfeeding tale after another.

The next time your dignity takes a nosedive, remember this: You are beautiful when you laugh. You are beautiful when you nurse. When the going gets tough, maybe you should try doing both at the same time.

A Bad Trip

Until I got things more or less figured out, there were times when breastfeeding made me feel like an awkward teenager. My body, or more accurately, my breasts, seemed to have minds of their own, and the harder I tried to maintain a thin veneer of control, the higher the odds were that things would take an embarrassing (and, in retrospect, hilarious) turn.

Age, patience, and experience are the most valuable currency in this motherhood game, and when you combine that with an unflappable sense of humor, you've reached billionaire status. Breasts leaking all over your brand-new business suit? Shrug your shoulders, laugh it off, and (as my daughter's preschool teacher is fond of advising her) *walk proud*. Migrating nursing pad making you look like a three-breasted monster? Do what I've had to do on more than one occasion: Hold your head high, stick your hand down your bra, and make the necessary adjustments. And *never forget to laugh*.

To say Cindi had her hands full would be putting it lightly. She and her husband had recently moved from Washington State to Arizona. She was in her early twenties, she'd just given birth to her second child, and—faced with the challenge of settling into a new house, understanding a new city, and caring for a newborn and a busy toddler—she felt on some days like her life was falling apart.

Then, one morning, Cindi's life really did fall apart, temporarily at least. She woke up to a crying baby and what she describes as a "gnarly" case of mastitis. She was running a high fever, and her infected breast was so sore that lifting her arm to nurse the baby brought tears to her eyes. Her toddler bounded out of bed and started running around the house, screaming for her attention. Sobbing, Cindi called her husband at his new job.

"I wanted him to come home and take care of the kids so I could go to the doctor," she recalls. "I'm not Mormon, nor had I ever known any Mormons, but as it turns out, the town we'd just moved to had a huge Mormon population. The boss's wife answered the phone—the boss and his family were Mormon. When I told her what was going on, she asked me if I was LDS."

Before continuing, Cindi explains that *LDS* is insider shorthand for The Church of Jesus Christ of Latter-Day Saints, the official name for the Mormon church: "Not being the religious type, but more the hippie type, I thought she was trying to ask me if I was on acid—*LSD*. I ended up yelling something like, 'No, I'm not on *acid*! I've got a bum boob and I need my freakin' husband to come assist my butt to the doctor!' She didn't understand about the acid—being all pure and all. So we were both highly annoyed at each other, but she finally sent my husband home to help with my boob."

"The moral of the story is this:" Cindi giggles, "When your boob hurts, don't call someone who thinks you are on acid."

Let It All Hang Out

A journalist and author of the sex memoir *The Edge of the Bed: How Dirty Pictures Changed My Life*, Lisa Palac isn't exactly what you'd call shy. She has written extensively about pornography and sexuality and even edited *Cyborgasm*, an electronic anthology of erotic stories, sexual scenes, and music. But when she was first learning to breastfeed her son, the forty-year-old Los Angeles resident realized that she still needed to work on feeling comfortable about the kind of full-frontal exposure that breastfeeding sometimes requires.

"Not long after my son was born, I decided I wanted to take him on an outing," Palac says. "I knew I'd have to nurse him in public, but because I wasn't that coordinated at it yet, I picked this café that's not particularly popular so I'd have some measure of privacy. When I got there, everything was perfect. Hardly anyone was there. I got something to drink, picked a quiet table in the corner, and decided to get to it. We were just getting settled with nursing when some guy walks into the café carrying a giant *iguana.* Remember, this was a practically empty café, but he picks the table right next to me and sits down with this huge lizard. Soon a crowd of about twenty people shows up to gawk at this guy's iguana, and here I am with my boob hanging out and milk spraying all over. I was dying, but thankfully everybody was too focused on the damn iguana to notice what I was doing."

For many mothers, the first weeks after the birth of a baby pass in a haze of diapers, interrupted sleep, and leaky breasts. Women who are used to leading busy lives suddenly find themselves marooned at home; a mother with a particularly demanding infant might end up, like Nancy, a thirty-six-year-old former television and video producer from Boston, "walking around the house for whole days wearing nothing but a nursing bra and sweatpants. I think I actually answered the door like that one time. I didn't realize what I was doing until the UPS man turned bright red."

But then the day comes when you're ready to leave the house. Maybe you have an obligation you can't put off, or maybe you realize that if you stay inside the house for *one more hour,* you're going to pull your hair out. Whatever the reason, you pack your fashionable new diaper bag, brush your hair, and pull together a nifty "transitional" outfit: maternity jeans (or stretchy pants), a big sweater, and a bright, distracting scarf. Then you dress your baby in something cute (another distraction: Look at the sweet little baby, not at her worn-out mama!) and bravely head out the door.

Once you are out in the world, you feel like a con just sprung from the can. The air is fresher and the sun is brighter than it used to be. Ordinary adult conversation is sexy, witty, and wonderful. You're gonna make it after all! You throw your beret in the air, Mary Tyler Moore–style, but as soon as it falls back down to earth, so do you. You realize that the beautiful baby you just strapped into her car seat is more delicate than a basket of eggs. You remember that you forgot to pack wipes. And you discover that the tummy-slimming leotard you just pulled on under your jeans is gonna make nursing a nightmare. What to do? My advice is this: Take a deep breath and (say it with me, now) *laugh.*

Once, back when my memories of being a new nursing mother were still fresh, I had a meeting with a woman in a busy downtown coffee shop. My coffee date, a writer I had never met before, brought her weeks-old son along to our meeting. At some point, the baby began to wail, making it clear that he needed to eat. It was summer, and this newly minted mother was wearing a knit tank dress—cute and comfortable, but not exactly *nursing* wear. I sympathetically watched her face fall when she realized that there was absolutely no modest way for her to put her son to her breast. While the baby rooted and began to whine, my companion laughed sheepishly, shrugged her shoulders, and rolled her eyes heavenward. Then she pulled the top of her dress over her shoulders and down to her waist, revealing a battered-and-splattered off-white nursing bra. Now mostly topless, she latched her baby and picked up the conversation where she left off. What else could she do? No one else in the coffee shop dared challenge this wild-eyed woman wearing nothing but a bra, and by exhibiting such good-natured bravery under fire, my new friend earned my lifelong respect.

Bridesmaids' dresses are rarely practical, but when you're a new nursing mother, they can present a particular challenge. They're never designed for easy access, and from what I hear, shiny polyester blends tend to stain when soaked with breast milk. In the course of my research, I've heard plenty of stories about lactating bridesmaids retreating to the bathroom, baby (or pump) in tow, but I had to laugh when Elizabeth, the freelance writer, recalled witnessing one maid with a much bolder approach to the no-access dress.

"When my sister-in-law got married, one of the bridesmaids had a four-week-old baby," Elizabeth says. "I remember watching her while she was sitting at the head table, and at some point late in the night, her baby was crying. She got this completely exhausted look on her face. She just reached up, unbuttoned a couple of buttons, and the whole top of her dress fell down. She sat there at the table in her bra, nursing."

"My first attempt at public breastfeeding was when I brought my oldest son in for his first appointment with the pediatrician," recalls Maja, the thirty-five-year-old newspaper reporter. "We were in the waiting room and he started fussing. I was still really new at this, and I was wearing a button-down shirt. So I unbuttoned it from the top— I hadn't figured out the unbutton-from-the-bottom trick yet—and it turns out I had to basically take my shirt all the way off just to get him to latch on. Worst thing about it was there was this young guy, maybe twenty-four years old, sitting directly across from me."

We all agree that breastfeeding women are beautiful, but no one—not even the most hard-core breast fetishist or committed La Leche League leader—can convince me that a nursing mother using a breast pump looks sexy, or even noble, for that matter. While breast pumps are a lifesaving invention, the sight of a woman with her tired boobies crammed into two clear-plastic funnels, her sorry, sore nipples pulled to ghastly lengths by a powerful sucking machine, isn't the kind of image that inspires artists to paint masterpieces. (More than once during my pumping-at-work days, I remember feeling something like thirty-three-year-old Amy, the online editor and nursing mother, who while taking photographs at a State Fair milking contest had the sudden, depressing realization that, "I'm not all that different from a cow.")

Dignity be damned. Sometimes, a mother has no choice but to mount her own personal pumping exhibition.

"Once I was on a business trip and I had a layover in La Guardia Airport," recalls the thirty-five-year-old radio producer Sasha. "I really needed to pump, and I literally couldn't find anywhere private to do it. Eventually, I ended up pumping in the women's bathroom by the sinks, right where all the other women in the airport were washing their hands. At that point my attitude was, 'Fuck it. This is a public health crisis.' I thought I was getting mastitis. I felt so hostile about it. I remember telling myself, 'If there's no outlet in the bathroom, I'll just plug the pump into a wall in the middle of the airport and wait until the security people come and get me.'"

What's in a Name?

Nurse a kid long enough, and eventually he'll come up with a name for your breasts. There's nothing wrong with this—you can't blame a guy for giving a name to something that important. But you might want to remember that while a nickname like "noonie" or "ba-ba" sounds cute at home, it could get embarrassing if, like one of the mothers I interviewed, you're over at Grandma's house one afternoon when your not-so-little bundle of joy starts unbuttoning your shirt, pulling up your bra, and yelling at the top of his precious little lungs, "Ta-ta time! Ta-ta *TIME*!"

Siri, the thirty-six-year-old museum curator, explains that her oldest child's *nip*name developed completely by accident. "When we first started learning the names for body parts, one day my son was pointing at my breasts and asking what they were," Siri recalls. "My husband was joking around for some reason and he said something like, 'Mama's a babe.' From that moment on, my son decided that *babe* was the word for breasts. And so that's what he decided to call them. He still does. The other day he asked me, 'Teachers have babes? Grandmas have babes?' I try to correct him, saying, 'No, the word is *breasts*,' but he still hasn't let go of *babe* yet."

As Maja's oldest son grew from a precious little baby into an active, verbal toddler, she discovered—too late—that children are anything but discreet.

"I made the age-old error of answering my son's questions about my anatomy," Maja laughs. "While we were nursing, he'd point at my breast and go, 'Da?' and I'd say, 'Nipple.' So that was the word he eventually started to use when he wanted to nurse. We'd be in a public place and he'd be like, 'Nip-ple. Nip-ple.' Then when he got a little older and his speech got a little clearer, it changed to, 'Have nipple!' and when he was really hungry, 'Have nipple *now*!' When my grandmother passed away a few years ago, we went to the funeral.

We were in this little country church, and suddenly my son started shrieking at the top of his lungs, 'Have nipple! HAVE NIPPLE *now*!'"

Now that her younger son is starting to talk, Maja is concerned that one day he might give her breasts a similarly embarrassing moniker. She wants him to know the correct words for different parts of the body—but she'd also like him to be a bit more subtle in his requests. So far, this young man seems to have come up with a decent alternative.

"When he wants to nurse, he says, 'Psst. Pssssst,'" Maja reports. "It feels a little bit better to me, a little less obvious, though some days it sounds like he's one of those dirty old men who stands on a street corner, trying to get your attention."

Welcome to the World

Alternative-parenting books are full of perky, well-meaning advice about how to create the ideal birth experience for your child. Rather than being abruptly pulled from the warm, comforting darkness of the womb into the sterile, bright light of a hospital room, a newborn, the experts advise, should experience birth as a quiet, gentle passage. Sure, *some* births work that way, but others, thanks in part to the miracle of modern medicine, fall far short of the incense-scented ideal.

No well-meaning mama should ever feel guilty if the fates intervene to make her child's birth a less-than-perfect experience. Take the case of Lisa Palac, the would-be iguana lover. Because of a pre-existing medical condition, she knew well ahead of time that her son would be born via a planned Cesarean. Palac was strongly committed to the idea of breastfeeding her baby, and after a lactation consultant told her that Cesarean babies sometimes have a hard time getting established at the breast, she set out to do everything she could to make that part of her child's birth experience move as smoothly as possible.

"Someone told me that when you have a Cesarean birth, you should try to breastfeed right there on the operating table, so your child doesn't have to make up for that transition later," Palac says. "But by the time I learned about that, it was fairly late in the game and my doctor said, 'No. You can't do it.' For some reason, I was panicked about that. I wanted my son to have at least *that* little bit of a normal birth experience."

Not all health-care providers discourage Cesarean mothers from breastfeeding on the operating table, but the policy at Palac's hospital was that mothers needed to go directly to a separate recovery room before being reunited with their babies. Left with no alternative, Palac concocted a plan to get her hands—not to mention her breasts—on her son as quickly as possible. While her husband and son were off getting acquainted in another part of the hospital, Palac was wheeled to the recovery room, accompanied by a close friend. Her hormone-fueled plan? With a bit of gentle support and encouragement from her friend, she'd get healthy in record time—and make a break for her baby.

"I was really pushing myself to recover so I could get to my son and nurse him as soon as possible," Palac says. "My friend said, 'Just relax and close your eyes. You'll be reunited soon.' I tried to listen to her advice, but I was really focused. After three hours, they finally agreed to take me back to my hospital room. The baby was there with his daddy. I was still a little weak, and someone had to help get him in my arms, but I was so excited. I thought: 'I can finally nurse!' I got settled, held out my arms, and said, 'Come on, little baby!' Then suddenly I was overcome by this great wave of nausea. It was a reaction to the drugs from the surgery. Someone grabbed a plastic tub and I barfed right in it! The funny thing is *I almost threw up all over my baby.* I laugh about it now, but what if I'd missed the tub and thrown up all over him? Imagine how much therapy he'd need to get over that."

What a Letdown!

Once we make it through the unpredictable puzzle that is puberty, women often come to believe that we have control over our bodies. If we maintain a healthy diet and exercise regularly, if we get enough sleep, if we have safe sex and always wear our seat belts, the theory goes, we'll keep ticking along like well-oiled machines straight through our twenties, thirties, and forties—until we hit fifty and make a date with menopause. For most of us, that's pretty much the way things go. We may have to deal with the occasional health crisis or personal tragedy, but we generally take it for granted that our bodies will work just like we want them to. But then, usually somewhere in that twenty-to-forty-year-old age range, biology kicks in and we decide to get pregnant. Talk about a curveball.

Even if you faithfully attend all the maternity aerobics classes you can squeeze into your schedule, there's no escaping the fact that for nine months, pregnancy transforms your body into a halfway house for a baby, a half-priced *pension* with a leaky faucet and a lumpy mattress. Once your baby is born, it's best to accept that things will still be out of control for much of the first few months. Having a baby is like one of those gut-the-house remodeling projects. It's dusty, messy chaos, with carpenters and plumbers and electricians leaving footprints all over the floor, but when it's finally done, you realize that it was all worth it.

In the beginning at least, most nursing mothers feel like their breasts have minds of their own. There's a point down the road when breastfeeding gets established, when most of us come to some sort of mutually agreed-upon arrangement with our mammaries, but at the beginning, breasts tend to want to assert their authority, springing a leak at the most awkward moments and tripping us up when we think we finally have them tamed.

"My oldest son was still pretty little when my husband and I went to a wedding," laughs Laura, the daily newspaper columnist and mother of two. "The ceremony was really emotional, and just after the bride and groom finished their vows, this amazing gospel choir burst into a beautiful rendition of 'Oh Happy Day.' Out of nowhere, I had this amazing letdown. I was wearing a sweater with a blazer over it, and suddenly I felt this little trickle. I looked at my lap, and my first thought was that I must've spilled some half-and-half or something. Then I realized it was coming from my breasts!

"As the song finished, people were getting up to leave. I was trying to adjust myself enough to make it out of the church, when I had another letdown. As I was subtly fixing my bra, my milk squirted out again and hit the guy in front of me right in the back of the head! I try to tell myself he thought it was the sprinkler system, because he looked up at the ceiling. Either that, or he was praying. I pretended I didn't have any idea what was going on. And the truth was, I *didn't*."

The Mama Advisory Board on Embarrassing Moments

- Unless you're aiming for maximum exposure, **avoid leotards, one-piece dresses, and tube tops,** says Cindi. "Any article of clothing that you have to completely remove in order for your kid to get access to your boob might be a bad idea."
- If pumping is a necessity, **make sure that you purchase a pump with an optional battery pack**—and make sure it's charged, suggests thirty-two-year-old account manager Kristin. "It really sucks if you get stuck somewhere where it's impossible to plug in your pump. It's better to be safe than sorry."

Chapter 6

Let's Talk about Sex . . . Or the Lack Thereof

Some people find pregnancy and breastfeeding sexy. For others, it's a major turnoff

They're attached to your body, you create the fuel for them, you feel the pleasure—and the pain—they produce, but there are times after the birth of a child when nearly every nursing mother wonders, *"Whose breasts are these anyway?"*

That feeling of booby dislocation may come from meeting the exhausting demands of a hungry infant. It may also come from having your breasts peered at, poked, and examined more than a stripper in a room full of sailors. Or you could be like me, who, while taking a bath on her first day home from the hospital, looked down and saw a pair of breasts suddenly so engorged, gravity-defying, and milk-filled that she looked (from the rib cage up at least) like a *Playboy* centerfold. "Where did *these* come from?" I asked my speechless husband.

Some new mothers end up feeling a bit like a Gold Rush mountain stream. When the cry goes up, "Thar's gold in them thar hills!"

hordes of prospectors—in the form of nurses, lactation consultants, well-meaning grandmothers, and, of course, a new infant—suddenly appear to stake their claim on a pair of ta-tas whose deed was formerly held by just one rightful owner. When a mother's milk guns begin to gear up for production, suddenly everyone thinks they can get in on the action.

Pre-baby, you likely saw your breasts as an extension of your sexual organs, something you shared (or didn't) with your sexual partners. Then you transformed yourself into a breeder, and your breasts were called upon to perform their biologically based duty. This was when things began to get confusing—on any number of levels.

It's not uncommon for a mother to feel like her newly "working" breasts have signed a chastity agreement, that they are now off-limits to anyone who is interested in them for anything beyond their nutritive qualities. This means amorous husbands or other sexual partners must adhere to a restrictive hands-off policy.

It may be that turning lactating breasts into an asexual—if functional—body part, something more akin to an elbow or a nose, is a completely normal and appropriate reaction. There are breast-feeding advocates who like to point out that in many parts of the world, including large parts of Africa and Asia, the female breast isn't viewed as a sexual body part. Other parts of a woman's body, like her behind or her waist or the nape of her neck, might be considered sexual, but breasts are reserved for feeding babies, and the notion that an adult male might get a thrill out of touching his partner's babyfeeders is enough to turn stomachs—the equivalent of requesting that your sweetie wear diapers and footie pajamas on your wedding night.

By transforming women's breasts into sexual objects, this argument continues, we Westerners have made the decision to breast-feed that much more complicated, adding disquieting levels of sexual innuendo to an act that has nothing to do with sexuality in the first place.

Nancy, the thirty-six-year-old former television and video producer from Boston, says that once her breasts were put to use feeding her child, she had a hard time thinking of them as anything but baby-feeders.

"Let's put it this way: Breastfeeding did not do wonders for our sex life," she laughs. "Prior to having my daughter, sex was an important part of my husband's and my lives in a way that it just isn't anymore. Having kids can put a crimp in your sex life anyway, and then breastfeeding just adds to that. I remember a friend saying that she told her husband after her son was born, 'These are for Alex now.' I remember thinking at the time that sounded strange, but then once my child was born, I remember thinking that these objects were now all about feeding the baby and they had nothing to do with my husband and sex. I was taken aback at how much I felt that way."

Nancy found that her interest in sex—and her willingness to share her breasts with her husband—slowly resurfaced after she weaned her daughter. "About six months after I stopped breastfeeding her, my sex drive returned," she reports. "In the end, I didn't have any residual 'hands-off' feeling, but I have to admit that it was slow to dissipate."

Penny Van Esterik, PhD, professor of anthropology at York University in Toronto, and a founding member of the World Alliance for Breastfeeding Action, says that the Western sexualization of the breast combined with cultural taboos surrounding children and sexuality make it difficult for nursing mothers to see their breasts as anything beyond asexual tools for baby nutrition. To make the leap from "pure" breastfeeding mother to "impure" sexual being crosses too many barriers, Dr. Van Esterik explains.

"I think that the heart of the difficulty is that the relationship between breastfeeding mother and infant can be interpreted as both nurturing *and* sexual," Dr. Van Esterik explains. "Breastfeeding blurs body boundaries. Where does one body end and another begin? If we really think about it, breastfeeding causes a complete shift in the way we look at the world, at our bodies and ourselves. Suddenly a woman is producing a food from a formerly sexual part of her body. Food designed for a baby comes from a zone formerly restricted to adults."

But there *are* perfectly normal women who find their lactating breasts to be a turn-on. Brenda, a forty-eight-year-old mother of one from Portland, Oregon, recalls the years she spent breastfeeding her now-preteen daughter as a time of great sexual awakening, an opportunity for her to appreciate her body's power and ability to be both sensual *and* nurturing.

"I never felt like breastfeeding diminished my sex drive in any way whatsoever," Brenda says. "When I was nursing, I felt like the fecund earth mother. If anything, breastfeeding *increased* my sex drive."

Brenda enjoyed the sensual feelings that breastfeeding aroused in her, and she never felt uncomfortable making the transition from sexual being to mother. In her mind, those barriers didn't exist, and she was able to fulfill both roles with little or no moral discomfort. "I think people with cultural hang-ups about breasts and sexuality may have a harder time incorporating those sexual, sensual, and maternal feelings," she says, "but I'm a looser kind of person than most women, and that wasn't an issue for me."

Lauren, a thirty-five-year-old editor and mother of one from Pennsylvania, discovered that her nursing breasts were actually more sexually responsive than they had been pre-baby. Immediately following the birth of her daughter, Lauren says that she experienced a brief "raw meat" time, where her body needed to rest and she had absolutely no interest in sex, but as the weeks and months wore on, her sexual feelings started to reappear.

"There was this turning point where I felt like I was getting more sleep, and my husband and I started to get much more active again," Lauren says. "At first the default was, 'Stay away from the breasts,' but then we started experimenting a little bit, and I found that my breasts actually were much more responsive than they had been before the baby. It was like a direct line from my nipple to my crotch. Any little tweak and it would be an instant orgasm. I was like, '*Score!*'"

When she first started breastfeeding, forty-year-old writer Lisa Palac daydreamed about a way she could use her milk-producing breasts as her own personal set of sex toys. "I had this fantasy about something that I wanted to do when my breasts were full of milk," she says. "I wanted to have sex with my husband and squirt my milk all over his face in the heat of passion. It seemed like a totally erotic, wanton thing to do."

But when the busy new mother actually found time to turn her fantasies into reality, her body just didn't cooperate. "By the time we finally got around to it," Palac admits sheepishly, "I didn't exactly gush like a human milk fountain. It was disappointing."

Now that most of you have thrown down your book in horror, pick it back up and understand that when it comes to sex, *variety is the spice of life.* While you (and not me, either—in case you were wondering) may not get off on the idea of soaking your partner in a milky-white shower, you have to understand that if it gets one well-intentioned gal goin', it can't be all bad. For Palac, embracing (and loving) the product of her own womanly body helped her reclaim her sexuality after the trauma of her son's birth. Her husband's willing-ness to help her make her (harmless) fantasy a reality showed love and commitment on his part. But you've gotta wonder if the poor guy wore a rain jacket.

Embracing Your Inner Freak

Juggling (or even merging) the roles of mother *and* sexual partner is tough. Don't let anyone tell you otherwise. Even women like Palac who make a living proclaiming their sexual liberation still get tangled up in the seemingly oppositional demands of *nurturer* and *nurturant.*

I look at it like this: If you're female, it's likely that you learned from an early age that a good mother gives up everything—even pleasure and self-satisfaction—for her child. But if you also like to think of yourself as a modern, liberated woman, and if you've watched even one episode of *Sex and the City,* you've probably absorbed the message that gals need to recognize their own inner horndogs and to demand satisfaction from their lovers (or at least learn how to satisfy themselves).

Then you went and had a baby, and suddenly those two images of the perfect woman are lining up for a head-on collision. No matter how hard you resist the decline into what you fear may be a dreary life of sexless motherhood, no matter if you have a full collection of vibrators and dirty magazines stashed in your bedside table, the day will likely come when a shrill church-lady voice will surface in the back of your mind just in time for a sharp jab of guilt and the question, "Is that any way for a *mother* to behave?"

While my advice is to give your inner church lady the heave-ho and embrace the fact that creating, giving birth to, and growing a baby is one of the most public celebrations of sexuality ever invented, I know all too well that even the sexiest of us can get caught up in the mama mind game. There are days when you catch a glimpse of your still-saggy belly in the changing-room mirror, when the guilt (and fatigue and self-doubt) is so strong that you might consider giving up on sex for good.

While many new mothers are distressed to find themselves feeling this way, it doesn't have to be a permanent condition. Remember: The road of life is long, and if you discover that the demands of early motherhood are dampening your inner flame, find solace in the thought that it only has to be a detour. Later, when you've caught up on your sleep, when your breasts stop leaking like a pair of worn-out faucets, you can pick up—older and wiser, undoubtedly—essentially right where you left off.

Robin, a stay-at-home mother from New Jersey, couldn't agree more. Now that her children are teenagers, she counsels nursing mamas who are worried that their sex lives have died on the vine to take a more patient, long-term look at sexuality:

"So what if you aren't all that interested in sex while you're

breastfeeding? I don't see that as a real problem. I know from experience that the interest eventually comes back. How long do you
nurse? A year, maybe two, right? It's not like twenty years of feeling
like the top half of your body is purely functional. I don't see it as a
negative. I see it as time off, as an opportunity to rediscover yourself
and rekindle your interest in your husband. That's a plus."

Palac may be more tuned in to her inner freak than most
women, but she's also a human being, and she's had to admit that
since she's become a mother, she doesn't always feel like a hottie.
Once the novelty of pregnancy and early motherhood had worn off,
she faced a new challenge to her sense of sexual identity: During her
pregnancy, Palac's weight ballooned from 130 to 200 pounds. After
her baby was born, she quickly shed thirty pounds, but as her son's
first birthday approached, she still had another forty to go.

The extra weight that had made Palac feel like a fertility goddess
during her pregnancy started to make her feel like a failure. Even
though she's smart enough to realize that many people think women
with a little meat on their bones are sexy, carrying around that extra
baby weight made Palac feel less than desirable. "I'm ashamed to say
it," she confesses, "but being fat doesn't help me feel sexy."

It takes a lot of guts for Palac to admit these feelings of self-
doubt. As a feminist, she believes that the pressure to live up to societal ideals of beauty is seriously damaging to women. She wants to
love herself—no matter what number appears on the scale. But there
are times when reality clashes with ideology.

I know how she feels. Intellectually, I buy the argument that a
post-baby body is a strong, accomplished body, but there were low
points early on when a glimpse of my suddenly unbabied profile
brought tears of frustration to my eyes. I hate to admit it, but in
those tender, early days, a long, hard look at my deflated torso could
make me feel like I'd poured a bucket of ice-cold water on my struggling libido. But eventually things changed, and the amazing restora-
tive effects of breastfeeding and baby-hefting kicked in. Before long,
I was back to my old self—an older, wiser version, perhaps, but every
bit as sexy as before.

"I have to believe that I'm beautiful and desirable," Palac says. "Right after my son was born, I remember trying to do some meditations on the beauty of my belly. I was like, 'I'm going to be gentle with you, belly, because my beautiful baby grew inside of you.' I had to work at being positive. My husband says, 'I can't take you criticizing yourself anymore. You've got to stop.' I responded, 'Then you need to tell me at least ten times a day how hot I am.'"

Not so long ago, Palac felt like an indestructible sex machine. Now there are days when she feels lumpy and vulnerable. "It's funny—and sad," she admits, "how quickly the tables have turned."

Worried that you'll never want to do the deed again? Sexuality experts counsel patience for new breastfeeding mothers. It takes time to get used to the changes your body is going through, but take it from me—and from countless others who've been through the baby fog and come out the other side: Your sex drive may flounder for a few months or weeks after your baby is born, but your old mojo *will* come back—maybe even mightier than before.

She Puts Out

Faulkner Fox, author of the parenting memoir *Dispatches from a Not-So-Perfect Life: Or How I Learned to Love the House, the Man, the Child,* has given the sexual implications of motherhood and breastfeeding some serious thought. Since giving birth to her two sons, she's written poetry and essays about the complicated expectations that often trip up modern mothers. She's even developed a performance-art piece on the subject titled *Sex-Talkin' Mama,* a recitation of her poems about motherhood and sexuality superimposed with a series of provocative images (a line drawing of an episiotomy, for instance) depicting the nitty-gritty of the mothering experience.

Fox has performed *Sex-Talkin' Mama* around the United States and Canada, at conferences and benefits, at a theater and a rape crisis center. Once, when she and her family were living in Austin, Texas, she taped the piece for the local public television station.

"After I was done with the taping, one of the tech guys, this old Texas guy, helped me carry some of my stuff out to the car," Fox recalls. "He'd seen my performance, watched the taping, heard my poems. As he was helping me get my stuff into the trunk, he turned to me and asked, 'Have you always been this horny?'"

To Fox, the Texas tech's reaction to her performance was indicative of the one-dimensional way society views motherhood and sexuality. There's only one acceptable way to be a mother. There's only one acceptable way to be sexual. Merging the two identities together—even in the most intellectual or artistic of formats—confuses people. They don't know what to say to a woman who willingly admits mixed feelings.

Fox's own experience of early motherhood and breastfeeding was different with both of her sons, but what each had in common was a period of time when she felt a certain ambivalence about sex—at least in the most traditional, heterosexual definition of *sexual intercourse*. She figures there's a pretty simple explanation for this.

"I was talking to a friend about different words that we use for sex," Fox says. "You know that expression people use when they think a woman or girl is easy? 'She puts out,' they say. In a way, when I was breastfeeding my babies, I felt like that expression described me, like I was *putting out* all day, like I was being sucked dry. By evening, I didn't have anything left to give, mentally or physically."

As Fox sees it, making the transition from sexual being to mother to sexual being *and* mother took time, and for many months following the birth of her sons, she had to grapple with a haunting feeling of dislocation. "A lot of what in the past—before my children's births—drove my sexual desire was being an intact, independent person during the day," Fox explains. "Then at night there was this desire to join with another person. When my children were still babies, when I had an infant suckling on me all day, I lost that daytime feeling of independence and intactness. In essence, I became two people occupying one body. At night, when my husband came home, instead of getting to the point of sexual desire, I had the desire to separate from everyone, to become my own person in whatever way possible."

Lately, Fox has wondered if a restrictive definition of intercourse may also play a role in mothers' decreased desire to quickly return to sexual activity after birth. The vagina and breasts, two areas that see active duty during birth and early motherhood, may just want to be left alone.

"In Western society," Fox says, "so much of sex is about men objectifying the breast or having vaginal intercourse in the way they want it. Maybe what a nursing mother wants is cunnilingus and nothing else. There's no reason a breastfeeding woman can't or shouldn't have an orgasm." Just having an orgasm isn't having sex in the way it's commonly defined, Fox explains. Ask Bill Clinton. "Having an orgasm rather than having heterosexual intercourse takes away the connections to ovulation or fear of pregnancy. Maybe if we expanded our definitions of sex and sexual activity, nursing mothers wouldn't come across as so disinterested in sex. Maybe we'd be more interested than ever before."

Going, Going, Gone

When I was a little girl, my parents subscribed to *National Geographic,* and because we were a rather modest family, the magazine served as my main source of information about what grown-up female breasts looked like. Sure, I'd seen women's breasts besides my mother's before, but mostly just for a few brief, embarrassed seconds in the locker room at the Y. And while these glimpses were fleeting, I could stare at the magazine for as long as I liked.

To tell the truth, those *National Geographic* women scared me. Their breasts, unadorned, asexual, working breasts, had a low-hanging, used-up look. Even though I had very little context in which to place these "foreign" bodies, I knew that I did not want to look like them when I grew up. I wanted breasts like the perky, mostly covered-up ones that I saw on TV, like Chrissy's on *Three's Company,* or Jill's on *Charlie's Angels.*

As I grew closer to womanhood, my breasts grew, too, and though they were responsible for a few embarrassing moments as an early-blooming preteen, I was mostly happy with them. They didn't point down to the floor, didn't deflate like a set of abandoned party balloons, and they didn't get in my way during my brief career on the high school track team. Later, when I was a full-fledged adult, they got their share of compliments from would-be (and real-life) lovers. My fear of one day waking up to a pair of *National Geographic* breasts was filed away as a distant, childhood memory.

Then my daughter was born, and once it was clear that I was breastfeeding her, well-meaning nursing mothers began to come out of the woodwork to tell me about the sorry state of their own breasts. "They'll never be the same," said my embittered-sounding neighbor. "They're pretty bad," confessed a gal in my book group. A dear friend had an even more brutal way of putting it: "They're all gone," she said, with a blunt, barking laugh. "Sometimes I miss them."

I'm a bit embarrassed to admit that all of this low-down, worn-out booby talk depressed me. Intellectually, at least, I want to redefine a nursing mother's altered breasts as strong, wise, and beautiful. But even though I was looking forward to becoming stronger and wiser, I still wanted my breasts to retain at least a tiny little bit of their former beauty. In the end, after my daughter was finished with me, my body made the transition back to a reasonable facsimile of its pre-baby form, and my breasts—never exactly centerfold-ready in the first place—returned more or less to their original, compact design. Whew. I dodged that bullet, I thought.

Then, four years later—and busy working on this book—I got pregnant again. After taking in my swelling form, many of the mamas I interviewed, especially the ones with more than one child, would get all sagelike on me, their voices taking on the husky, cigarette-tinged tone of *been-there-done-that* gals. They sounded almost gleeful when they'd assure me that the first kid was just a warm-up. The second child was the one that *really ruined their breasts*. Sara, a twenty-nine-year-old mama of two from Pennsylvania, even provided this chilling description of her post-baby boobs: "It looks like someone took a handful of skin and yanked them down: They're just hanging there, all emptied out."

For now, I prefer to shut my ears to such comments and soldier on. Till the second one's fully cooked and eating graham crackers, I'm gonna tell myself that the jury's still out, that no matter what happens, I'll continue (in my own low-key way) to appreciate my *feminine appendages*—especially after they've done their womanly duty.

Once her children were weaned, author Faulkner Fox was so disturbed by the state of her "sucked-dry" mammaries that she wrote a poem. She titled it "What Has Happened to My Breasts?"

"When I first started complaining about the condition of my breasts, my husband would say to me, 'I don't understand why you let this bother you,'" Fox says. "In my poem I respond, 'If you woke up and half your dick was gone, you'd be upset, too.'"

Now Fox's sons are older, and she has had years to come to terms with her changed body. A low-sugar diet combined with the toning power of yoga have made her smaller breasts look less out of place on her leaner, more muscular torso. Now, when she thinks about her negative reaction to her post-childbearing body, she understands that it signified a deeper, psychological subtext: In this culture, breasts are a big part of our sexual identity. When our breasts suddenly resemble our *mothers'* breasts, we may feel like we've lost power, sexual currency, or even an essential part of our womanhood.

"Nobody told me that this would happen," Fox says. "When it did, I felt betrayed. I didn't expect that after I nursed my sons, my breasts would be half the size they were before I nursed. I didn't like the sucked-out look that they had taken on. I don't know if that means that I'm superficial, but I just didn't like the feeling it gave me, like I had been used up and discarded."

To varying degrees, other women have shared Fox's sense of betrayal. Newspaper reporter Maja says one look at her post-baby breasts reminded her of her older female relatives.

"People never told me that after breastfeeding, your boobs shrink," Maja says. "Now, the whole texture of my breasts is different. Somehow you have to learn to accept the fact that these once-nubile, blossomy, perky little things are never coming back. I'm Finnish, and I'd seen my grandmother and my mother and my aunts naked in the sauna. I remember being in my twenties and thinking, 'How did that happen to their breasts?' And then I went through childbirth and nursing, and suddenly mine look sort of like theirs did. At times it's depressing."

Radio producer Sasha points her index fingers downward when she explains the state of her breasts. "Now, I've got these hanging nipples," she laughs. "I swear they never used to be that way. My husband calls them my 'sad little milkers.'"

Lisa Palac is still coming to terms with her baby-changed body. In her wistful memories, her "innocent, unused" breasts symbolize pure beauty, something she took for granted before it was gone. "They used to be so up, up, up," Palac says a bit wistfully. "Now they are down, down, down."

In contrast, breastfeeding two children has made Betsy's already hefty breasts grow even larger than they were before. While she's had to make some necessary wardrobe adjustments to accommodate her bulkier new companions, this thirty-six-year-old freelance writer and mother of two from Arlington, Virginia, insists that the change has had some side benefits. "Our sex life may not be back anywhere close to where it was before the kids were born," she laughs, "but the new, improved breasts have been a good distraction. My husband certainly hasn't minded these triple Fs."

Though breastfeeding often ends up reducing the size of a woman's breasts, some formerly flat-chested women have found that nursing caused their cup size to increase—even after their children were weaned. I've also been told of mamas who encouraged their babies to nurse for *years,* simply because they appreciated the fringe benefit of an ampler bosom.

Robin from New Jersey and Lauren from Pennsylvania were surprised to find that nursing actually made them feel better about their breasts than they did before their children were born. For Lauren, it was the powerful realization that this part of her body could be both sexual and nourishing. For Robin, it was the sense of accomplishment she still feels every time she catches a glimpse of her breasts in the mirror.

"They might be a little lopsided now, but for a woman my age they're still looking pretty good," she says. "And they fed my babies and kept them healthy. I'm proud of what they did, and that makes me like them even more than I did before."

The Daddy Factor

Let's take a moment to consider the fathers. If you are married to—or partnered with—your baby's daddy, it's likely that he has had to make a few adjustments of a sexual nature since you gave birth to his child. Up until this point, your man may have thought that he held his own personal time-share on your breasts. But now that Baby is busy staking her claim over the territory, Daddy will likely have to move over and contend with your shifting perceptions of your breasts' proper use.

And even if having your boobies fondled by someone other than your baby doesn't exactly turn your stomach, a day spent feeding, burping, and diapering may be enough to transform even the hottest potato into a cold fish. For a few months at least, the only thing you might want to do when you hit the sheets is sleep. For many couples, negotiating a comfortable set of ground rules for post-baby sexual interaction can require open communication, respect for the mother's feelings—and, some might say, the patience of a saint.

Todd Seabury-Kolod, an early-childhood education instructor and father of two, says that breastfeeding is "definitely a dry period for many couples. I remember that my wife often used the phrase, 'touched out.' All that nurturing really dries the well."

Seabury-Kolod teaches a parenting class for fathers. Often new dads tell him that immediately following a baby's birth, they struggle to understand just what their role is in their family. Because nursing mothers and their infants are by necessity so closely connected, and because mothers tend to devote every ounce of their energy to their newborns, fathers can feel left out in the cold—both physically and metaphorically.

"In my dads' class, some fathers talk about how they don't really feel all that comfortable with kids between birth and three months," Seabury-Kolod says. "They can't relate to young infants the way mothers can. They don't have that nursing bond, for one thing, and that makes for a sense of detachment. Add that to the limited intimacy experienced between mothers and fathers at that time, and many men really begin to feel like they are out of the loop." Many men see sex as a way of reconnecting with their partners, of strengthening bonds and communicating feelings of love and deep attachment, Seabury-Kolod explains. Even if a man has an intellectual understanding of why the woman in his life isn't all that keen about *getting it on,* her lack of interest in sex can feel like a slap in the face.

Patrick, a married father of two from Minneapolis, adds that bringing a child into the world causes a disruption in everyone's life. For weeks after the birth of his children, he felt like he was walking on eggshells, trying to understand just what his wife wanted from him. And when it came to sex, he had no idea what to do.

"Most men—even the most sensitive ones—don't have much experience talking openly about their sex lives," Patrick says. "We have a hard time communicating our needs. With my wife, it took me a few months to understand that the best thing to do was to back off a little bit, to try to stay in tune with her feelings and understand when she was feeling the most energetic. I tried to pay attention to her ebb and flow. Once I got that down, things started to feel more normal."

Patrick says that following the births of both of his children, he felt a strong, almost primal attraction to his wife. She felt the same way about him, but it took her longer to be ready to go there. Somewhere deep inside, both of them felt a need to reconnect, to share the powerful experience of birth. Sure, on one level, Patrick's desire was about sex, but it was also about something deeper, and so he bided his time until his wife was ready to welcome him back into her arms.

While Patrick knows men who are turned on by the sight of a nursing mother, it doesn't work that way for him. "I'm not turned off by watching my wife breastfeed," he says, "but for me, the turn-on is the renewed excitement about my marriage and my family life. It's much more about my libido being increased by entering an exciting new phase of life, with the person I love most in the world."

Can You Feel It?

Unless they're swearing *never to have it again in their entire goddamn lives,* sex is the last thing many women want to think about when they're in the middle of labor. But the truth is that there is a connection between sex and childbirth—beyond the obvious cause-and-effect relationship.

Clearly, those of us who got pregnant the old-fashioned way understand at a base level the old adage *what goes in must come out.* Depending on the size of your nine-months-pregnant belly, the *must come out* part can be a frightening prospect. I've been through it twice, and I'm not gonna lie to you: Labor hurts. But natural childbirth advocates (and you can count me among them) maintain that a drug-free birth can also be a source of pleasure—on an emotional ("I did this!") and even physical ("I did this and it felt amazing!") level. Anyone who tells you that the experience of drug-free labor is like one extended orgasm, however, is out of her mind, but there *is* a powerful sensual pleasure to it, an experience to remember for the rest of your life.

Breastfeeding advocate Marsha Walker is willing to go even further: "A birth without any medication—talk about a rush! *Oooooooh!* When you push that baby out all by yourself, you feel such incredible power and pleasure."

That feeling of ultimate body mastery, of indescribable power and pleasure, can also be achieved through breastfeeding, Walker believes. She argues that when we set our bodies free to do what they are designed to do, when we avoid unnecessary medical interventions that can dull our sensations and take the power out of our hands, women leap to a whole new level of sensual knowledge and understanding.

"Giving birth is like the most amazing sexual experience you've ever had," adds Lauren from Pennsylvania. "It's all-consuming, it's elemental on a level that you have never experienced before. In order to give birth without medication, you have to be a completely physical person. You're not cerebral at all in that moment. And that's what good sex is like, too. It's getting out of your head altogether and really getting lost in the moment. It hurts, but it also feels *good.*"

While Walker understands that epidurals and other pain medications are helpful tools to assist women in labor, she also believes that their widespread use has robbed many women of the sense of accomplishment that comes with a natural birth. Automatic formula-feeding has a similar effect, Walker argues. When a woman is not encouraged to at least attempt feeding her child from the breast, she is given the message that what comes from her body is inferior, that the natural sensations it experiences and the fluids it produces should be dulled and disposed of.

"The sensation of birth has been taken away from most women," Walker says. "A lot of women are so afraid of giving birth that they don't want to feel it. We now have hospitals with a 98 percent rate of epidurals. Approaching labor and parenthood that way gets us into a situation we call 'painless parenting.' You get into this point where you don't want anything about being a parent to hurt. You don't want feeding your baby to hurt, so you are going to bottlefeed. You don't want leaving him to hurt, so you put him in day care from day three. You don't want sleep to hurt, so you shut your baby in a crib and ignore his cries. It goes on and on. But being a parent isn't painless. We fool ourselves when we believe it can be."

For me, breastfeeding was never a *Penthouse Forum*-level turn-on, but I *will* admit that discovering my ability (imperfect as it was) to feed my child from my own breasts served as an eye-opening acknowledgment of my body's power and prowess. When I combined that with the mind-blowing experience of helping my wet, slippery daughter come barreling into the world, I couldn't help but feel like a studly marathon runner, a hot potato who understood her body's abilities and desires even better than she had before.

Author and therapist Jane Swigart, PhD, says that no matter what decisions a mother makes in the birth, care, and feeding of her child, the relationship that's forged between mother and infant carries sexual/sensual overtones that cannot—and should not—be denied. If she refuses to acknowledge this reality, a mother essentially blocks her ability to understand her own capacity for healthy sexual arousal and recovery.

"Letting go and accepting the feelings that wash over us in early motherhood is the key to a healthy re-entrance into the adult world from the overwhelming world of infancy," Dr. Swigart says. "Maternal love and sensual awareness are not polar opposites. They are emotions that naturally enhance and support one another."

Brenda, who describes herself as "a real granola head," can't help but agree with Dr. Swigart's advice. "I thought that pregnancy and breastfeeding were the most special things in the world," she says. "I used to say that pregnancy was this internal mystery. For nine months, this baby just grew inside me, and then when it came out, breastfeeding became the most wonderful thing in the world. When you are nursing, every day you see your baby grow and thrive, thanks to something that you are providing for her. It makes you feel like a woman in a woman's body. And what could possibly be sexier than a strong woman's body doing what it's designed to do?"

The Mama Advisory Board on Sex

- **Don't worry if sex seems like a turnoff right now,** says Robin. "This dry period is only one part of your life. If you don't feel like you're in the mood right now, have faith that you will be again sometime in the future. The feelings come back—usually after you start getting enough sleep."

- **"Try really listening to your body,"** Brenda says. "Relax, take a deep breath, and forget about what people are telling you to think and feel. If you take time to savor the sensations of early motherhood, you just might discover that it's really a very sensual, maybe even sexual time."

- This one's for the daddies: **Patrick suggests that partners pay special attention to their breastfeeding babe's changing moods:** "With my wife, I tried to focus on how she was feeling day to day, hour to hour. I tried to sense when she was in the mood to be intimate instead of focusing on when *I* wanted to be. I tried to step back and really listen to her cues."

Chapter 7

Ouch!

There ARE times when breastfeeding just doesn't work. When that happens, it hurts—in more ways than one

Once and for all, let's clear something up: With help, advice, and patience, almost all biological mothers *can* breastfeed. But in a few cases, some can't.

There was a time in the not-so-distant past—maybe even during your own infanthood—when mothers were routinely told that they did not make enough milk to feed their babies. Doctors and nurses, convinced of formula's scientifically tested superiority and unsurpassed modernity, would actively encourage anxious parents to switch from breast to bottle. In confident, often condescending tones, mothers were told that the best food for their infants was the *man*-made stuff, not the natural, *woman*-made food. Handing a worried mother a bottle was much easier (at first, anyway) than taking the time to make breastfeeding really work.

Today the message has changed. Most doctors and nurses have jumped on the "breast is best" bandwagon, and there's a fairly universal acceptance of the fact that breast milk is superior to formula. Scientific studies supporting the benefits of mothers' milk have been widely reported by most news media, and public health campaigns are full of information about the developmental advantages enjoyed by breastfed infants. Breastfeeding, the experts say, is good for your baby, good for you, and good for society.

This dramatic attitude adjustment is, to be certain, a positive development. How can it not be? But if you are a woman who has tried and for one reason or another cannot make breastfeeding work, swimming against the current of popular opinion and joining the ranks of the formulafeeders can make you feel like a failure, or even worse, a bad mother.

Obviously, not everyone in this country looks down on mothers who choose formula over breast milk. In fact, most American parents still feed their babies formula at some point in their lives. But the pro-nursing crowd is gaining ground, and if you fit a certain demographic (over thirty, educated, middle-to-upper income), the pressure to choose breast over bottle can get pretty intense.

What's life like for a mama who, by all measures, fits the breastfeeding profile, but who for some reason can't make breastfeeding work?

"Let me tell you, it's a bad spot to be in," says Gail from Manhattan Beach, California. A traumatic Cesarean birth combined with an intense, early case of mastitis set the thirty-eightyear-old former entertainment attorney running for her local supermarket's formula aisle when her daughter was still a newborn. Though her baby seemed to be healthy and happy on a mostly formula diet, Gail felt bothered enough by her own guilt and what she perceived as "judgmental" looks from other mothers to launch her own aggressive relactation campaign. She battled through seven more bouts of mastitis and pumped more than an overworked heifer until her daughter finally made the switch to 100 percent breast milk.

"I'm incredibly glad I did it," Gail says. "But sometimes I wonder where all of my motivation was really coming from. Why did I feel like such a failure when breastfeeding didn't seem like it would work for me? Why did I have to bend over backward just to nurse? Someone once told me that *any* mother who tries hard enough can breastfeed. Maybe I didn't want it to look like I wasn't trying hard enough."

If you surveyed all formulafeeding mothers, you'd certainly find plenty who simply preferred bottle to breast, but ask a few more questions, and you'd find yet another group sitting uncomfortably off to one side. They're the mamas who realize that while formula may not be the best possible option for their babies, for them it is the *only* option. Sprinkled in this group are mothers who more than anything wanted to breastfeed, but for any number of reasons (adoption, breast reduction, health problems, or an unsupportive work environment, to name a few) can't. Some are able to nurse their children part-time; others pump and supplement and consult for months before finally giving up. Still others, like Gail, eventually manage to make the switch from bottle to breast—overcoming obstacles that would make most mothers run for the hills. No matter what their personal histories are, these in-between mothers are a guilt-wracked bunch, and when you take time to hear their stories, I'll wager that you'll cut them some much-needed slack.

Her Cup Runneth Over

To put it bluntly, Michelle was sick and tired of her breasts. Through puberty, adolescence, and early adulthood they grew and grew and grew, until she felt overwhelmed by the sheer size and weight of the two protuberances attached to the front of her torso. Because they were cumbersome and awkward, Michelle's breasts kept her from being as physically active as she wanted to be, made buying clothing a chore, and drew unwanted attention from men and curious adolescent boys.

"More than anything, I wanted to get rid of my boobs," Michelle says, wearily. "And so, as soon as I could, I did."

When Michelle was twenty-two years old, she underwent breast-reduction surgery. At the time, it felt like the best decision she ever made. "Suddenly I could run. I could wear cute clothes," she says. "I didn't have a serious boyfriend at the time, so I wasn't even thinking about motherhood. Before the surgery, the surgeon and his nurse came to me and said, 'After this procedure, if you want to have babies someday, you may not be able to breastfeed.' I didn't let that deter me. I thought, 'If I ever have children, I'll figure the breast-feeding part out then. Just cut 'em down to size!'"

In the years since her surgery, Michelle's life has changed. Now thirty years old, she fell in love and got married. She started a successful career in health-care sales, and somewhere along the way decided to start a family. She loved her remodeled breasts, and for years she didn't give nursing a second thought—until she became pregnant with her first child. Once she began to feel her baby move inside her womb, Michelle realized that she really wanted to breastfeed this child—if at all possible.

"Maybe it was a pregnancy hormone thing, but the prospect of nursing suddenly became very appealing to me," Michelle recalls. "Of course there was the obvious nutritional benefit, and then there was the economic benefit of not buying formula, but the most appealing thing by far was the idea of nourishing my child from my body."

Her surgeon's warning lurking in the back of her mind, Michelle decided to find out just how likely it was that her now "small and petite" breasts would ever be able to produce milk. After a quick Web search, she discovered BreastFeeding After Reduction (BFAR), a nonprofit organization that supports nursing mothers who have undergone breast-reduction surgery.

What Michelle read on www.bfar.org wasn't all that encouraging. Even if a woman's surgeon is sincerely concerned about retaining her future ability to breastfeed, the BFAR experts warned, because breast reduction involves the removal of breast tissue, there is always a possibility that after surgery a woman's breasts will not be able to produce enough milk to nourish an infant. Most post-reduction mothers need to at least supplement their infants with formula.

"Although we do not have statistics available that provide outcome percentages, we do know that after working with hundreds of mothers to help them breastfeed after [breast-reduction] surgery, only a very, very small fraction of these moms have been able to breastfeed without supplementation. Most do not have a full milk supply," the BFAR site cautions. "We urge you not to be lured into thinking that you could beat the overwhelming odds. If you have the surgery before you have your babies, you will almost certainly have to supplement."

Still, Michelle was determined to find out if she would be among the "very, very small fraction" of post-reduction mothers who can breastfeed exclusively. From the beginning of her pregnancy, her body began to give off hopeful signs. For one thing, her breasts felt like normal pregnant breasts. "They seemed like they were filling out and doing what they needed to do to prepare for lactation," Michelle recalls. When her son was born, she immediately put him to her breast, and "he latched on right there in the hospital."

Heeding BFAR's advice, Michelle tried to be realistic about the amount of milk her breasts could produce: "From the start, I was making a little milk, and I was really encouraged by that, but I didn't want to be one of those mothers who felt so guilty about doing anything but breastfeeding that her baby ended up starving. So I supplemented him from the very beginning."

Like Michelle, BFAR cofounder Diana West, a certified lactation consultant and author of *Defining Your Own Success: Breastfeeding After Breast-Reduction Surgery*, had reduction surgery when she was in her twenties. When she became pregnant with her first child, she assumed she would not be able to breastfeed him, but after he was born, West says she was overcome with a "mother tiger" impulse that inspired her to put him to the breast. What she discovered surprised her.

"Most doctors who do breast reductions either tell moms that they won't be able to breastfeed at all after the surgery or that there won't be any problem," West says. "Neither one of these is completely true. While almost all post-reduction mothers *do* have a reduced milk supply—especially with a first baby—most can produce some amount of breast milk. While I produced some milk for my first child, I did not have enough to feed him exclusively. But with my second and third babies I had a full supply."

In the months following her first son's birth, Michelle focused on increasing her milk supply. She gave the baby some formula, but she also pumped several times a day as well as feeding him at the breast. When she returned to work after a three-month maternity leave, she brought a pump with her, taking several pumping breaks each day. Still, Michelle was never able to make enough milk to drop formula completely.

"I felt bad about that, for sure," Michelle says, "but it wasn't like nobody warned me ahead of time." She tried to make up for the lack of breast milk simply by holding and comforting her son as much as possible, by making the act of bottlefeeding as intimate as time at the breast was.

"It's important for all mothers to realize that the only option isn't perfection—or nothing at all," West emphasizes. "You are not a failure if you cannot breastfeed exclusively. Anything you can do for your baby—any amount of breast milk you can give him—is fabulous and much more than most people do."

La Leche League International supports Michelle's approach of combining breast and bottle for post-reduction mothers. "The physical act of breastfeeding is more than the quantity of milk that is supplied, as you will find once you hold your baby in your arms," the organization states on its Web site, www.lalecheleague.org. "Breastfeeding is warmth, nutrition, and mother's love all rolled into one. Understanding and appreciating the signs of knowing when your baby is getting enough to eat is one of the most important things a new mom can learn, whether the mom has had breast surgery or not."

Like many mothers, Michelle never enjoyed pumping, and putting so much work into something with so few rewards quickly became frustrating. "While I was home on maternity leave, I tried to breastfeed my baby all the time," Michelle says. "When I returned to work, I still needed to pump, and because I was pumping I could watch as my output diminished. Sometime after six months, when it became too much work for the paltry amount I was producing, I just quit."

Michelle's second child presented another set of problems.

"I had the same intention to breastfeed with supplementing like I did with my older son," Michelle says. "I went in with more experience, and so I thought I knew the drill, but this baby never latched. Looking back at it, I'm sure that if I had tried harder, he eventually would've latched, but I figured I knew how things were going to go with my breasts from the last time, and I didn't think it was worth it to struggle with the latch *and* the pumping. We started giving him a bottle right away, and I started pumping as soon as my milk came in."

After three months of pumping and bottlefeeding, Michelle was able to produce only one four-ounce bottle of breast milk a day. The lower production probably had a lot to do with the fact that Michelle's breasts weren't getting direct stimulation from her infant: Many mothers see that their breasts produce less milk when stimulated by a pump than they do when stimulated by a child. With two children to care for and the end of her maternity leave looming on the horizon, Michelle decided to stop pumping. When she was done, she tossed the pump and never looked back.

"A lot of my memories of that second maternity leave are of sitting on my bedroom floor with pumps over both of my nipples," Michelle sighs. "It was the middle of the summer, and I'd have the air conditioner on and I'd be pumping away and feeling really sorry for myself. After a while it got to the point where I felt like I was taking time away from being with my baby just to spend all of my time pumping out these sorry little bottles of milk. It got so it didn't seem like a worthwhile trade."

There were times, especially with her littlest boy, when Michelle says she felt self-conscious about feeding him with a bottle. People make assumptions based on your preferred method of infant feeding, she says, and some days it drove her crazy to imagine that a breastfeeding mother assumed she was lazy, selfish, or careless when she whipped out a bottle in public.

"I remember wanting to explain myself a couple of times," Michelle says. "I don't remember facing direct disapproval, like someone saying something nasty to me at the mall, but I was aware that people could misconstrue the fact that I was feeding my four-month-old a bottle with the idea that I didn't care to breastfeed. But that really wasn't my case at all, and unless I told them, complete strangers were likely to make that assumption."

West, whose Maryland-based lactation practice often assists mothers with low milk supply, says that she would advise a young woman considering breast reduction to hold off on the surgery until after she has had children. "I really understand how difficult it can be to have really large breasts," West says. "It's not only physically painful but emotionally painful as well. But it is also a very difficult road to attempt to breastfeed when you don't have a full milk supply."

Despite her struggles, Michelle says she wouldn't do anything differently. Not the pumping and the partial formulafeeding—but most of all not the surgery. "The surgery changed my life for the better," she says. "It's true that it made nursing more difficult than it had to be, but we worked that out. In the end, I came away thinking I did what was best for me—and what was best for my children."

About Face

Julie loved to breastfeed. Like many women, she wasn't all that enthusiastic about nursing before she became a mother. But once her daughter was born and the nurses at her hospital gave her a crash course on the basics of breastfeeding, thirty-six-year-old Julie became a convert. Overnight, she turned into one of those mothers who will talk at length about the benefits of nursing, a woman who proudly links her child's good health to the natural antibodies found in her breast milk. Julie loved many things about being a mother, but breastfeeding was always at the top of her list.

"We had a great experience," Julie recalls. "I loved nursing my daughter so much that I really felt like an activist about it. I wanted everyone to do it. After my maternity leave, I went back to work three days a week at a big bank in Minneapolis, and when I was at work, I'd carry my pump around with pride. I didn't care what people thought. I'd pump three times a day, even in unlocked conference rooms with my back to the door. I felt indignant if someone tried to come in or if my work schedule interfered with my pumping schedule. I was like, 'Don't mess with me. I've got more important things to do.'"

Julie's little girl nursed until she weaned herself at seventeen months. A year later, Julie happily became pregnant again. When a routine ultrasound revealed that their son had a bilateral cleft lip and possibly a cleft palate, the family's life was turned upside down.

Like most people, Julie and her husband knew very little about cleft babies. As soon as possible, Julie sat down at her computer and began to research the condition. While she quickly learned that cleft lips and palates are a relatively common birth defect (they occur in one of every 700 births), and that they can be repaired through a series of simple reconstructive surgeries, Julie also discovered that breastfeeding a cleft baby can present a particular challenge. This was a blow that she wasn't prepared for.

"One of the first things I mourned was that I wasn't going to be able to nurse this baby," she says. "I had so many fond memories of my daughter's beautiful cupid's-bow baby mouth, and I knew that with this child we weren't going to have this. And then I learned that it was going to be close to impossible to breastfeed my son. I realized I had my work cut out for me."

Julie read conflicting information about breastfeeding cleft babies. "Some people will tell you that if you put the baby on your breast and put your thumb over the cleft lip, the baby can suck," she says, "but there are so many cases of that not working, of babies not getting enough food that way." Cleft experts explain that the odds of successfully breastfeeding a baby born with lip or palate deformities are low. It is true that some cleft babies—especially those with intact palates—can be breastfed, but the percentage of successful cases remains small.

Eventually, Julie found an online group for parents of cleft babies through the cleft support and advocacy organization Wide Smiles (www.widesmiles.org). "A woman there said, 'Forget feeding at the breast. Pump milk and bottlefeed. Don't set yourself up for failure. Your baby is not going to thrive if you insist on the breast,'" Julie says. "I didn't want to face that, so I pumped."

Because Julie's son had both a cleft lip *and* palate, she felt convinced that he would never be able to nurse at the breast. Instead, Julie and her husband invested in a set of Haberman Feeders, bottles designed especially for cleft babies and others who have a hard time sucking. When she took her son home from the hospital, Julie borrowed two hospital-grade breast pumps and established a doctor-approved "'round the clock" schedule of pumping and feeding, pumping and feeding. Thanks to his mother's tireless devotion, her boy was on exclusive breast milk for almost five months, but the effort required to maintain the family's stockpile of the stuff eventually began to wear on the entire household. Eventually Julie switched over to formula.

"It took a massive amount of sleep deprivation to finally knock me to my senses," she says. "It quickly became clear that when I was pumping, I just wasn't able to produce as much milk as I did when I had an actual baby latched on. So I'd have to pump forever just to get enough for the baby to eat, and then it would take him anywhere from thirty to fifty minutes for him just to eat an ounce. It seemed like that was all I was doing. It was making me insane."

Since his birth, Julie's son has thrived through a series of surgeries and is now well on his way to full facial repair. ("He's always been a happy baby," Julie says proudly. "He's a real trooper.") But there are times when Julie still feels a keen sense of loss, when she thinks about the intimate, bonding moments she missed with her son. Sometimes she even wonders how this loss will affect his future development.

"For a long time, I really felt like a bond was ripped away from both of us," Julie admits, "that somehow he wouldn't feel as close to me as his sister does. Breastfeeding my daughter was such a loving, close thing, and I felt sad that I wasn't going to have that with him."

On the other hand, Julie realizes that she has made choices that have allowed her to have time with her son that she'd never had with her daughter. She quit her job to stay home and care for him through all of his surgeries and recovery. "I've been there for him every minute. Maybe the bonding issue was not as big a deal as I thought it would be. Maybe it was more a loss on my side than it was on his. He doesn't know any differently."

Once, Julie confessed her feelings to a breastfeeding friend. "I'll never forget this," she recalls. "What she said to me was, 'Look around. There are many intelligent, wonderful people who drank formula.' It sounds so obvious, but it really helped me to hear someone say that, because I felt so awful about stopping."

What Julie's friend had to say is important, West says, but Julie also shouldn't dismiss the positive benefits of all the wonderful breast milk her son ingested during his first five months of life. To continue to pump for so many months is a great accomplishment. In her own practice, West says she always tries to acknowledge the gift her clients have given their babies, because she believes that breast milk—even in small amounts—has lasting, positive effects.

"I celebrate every drop of breast milk that a baby gets," West says. "It's much better than nothing. In fact, it's amazing. It's a gift that lasts a child for their whole life."

Running on Empty

If anyone fit the profile of a successful breastfeeder, it would be Monika, a thirty-eight-year-old magazine editor from San Francisco. When she got pregnant, she found herself a midwife and planned a home birth. She read up on breastfeeding, talked to nursing friends, and invested in a high-quality, efficient pump. Then her son came hurtling into the world, announcing his arrival with a grueling labor that began in Monika's house and ended more than a day later in a hospital delivery room.

"After fifteen hours of labor at home, I told the midwife, 'I don't think I can do this myself,'" Monika recalls. "So we went to the hospital. I was in active labor for thirty hours before he was finally born. I have never been so exhausted in my entire life. I was seeing double,

I was so wiped out." After the birth, mother and baby caught up on their rest, sleeping almost constantly and taking only the occasional break to meet with the hospital lactation consultant. While the baby found his way to the breast, he had what Monika describes as a "wimpy" latch, a problem she wrote off as a by-product of sleepiness and maybe a touch of jaundice.

Because she had done her homework, Monika spent the first days after her son's birth anticipating engorgement. She had read that when their milk comes in, most mothers feel like their breasts are filled to bursting. While Monika's breasts felt slightly fuller, she says she never felt anything even close to what's described in books.

"For a while, I thought maybe it was just taking me a little longer than normal to get going," Monika says, "but as the days passed, nothing really changed."

A few days after discharge, Monika's hospital sent a nurse to do a routine check on mother and baby. When the nurse noted that the baby hadn't gained any weight since going home, Monica feared her milk hadn't come in: "She took one look at me and said, 'Your milk's in.' I asked, 'What happened to the engorgement?' She said, 'Some women just don't get engorged.'"

So Monika kept trying to nurse her son, though as the days passed it began to feel more and more frustrating. "He would latch only for so long and then he'd quit," Monika recalls. "Then he'd get fussy. It turns out he'd quit sucking when there wasn't any more milk coming. At first, I thought he was just lazy or sleepy. In retrospect, I realize he's not a dumb baby. He didn't want to waste his energy."

Monika wanted to breastfeed her baby more than anything, but she also wanted him to be happy and healthy. Healthy babies are supposed to gain weight. If her son wasn't gaining, then there must be something wrong. So Monika set up an appointment with a lactation consultant, who suggested that she take a variety of herbs known for their ability to stimulate milk production. The lactation consultant encouraged Monika to stick with exclusive breastfeeding for a few more days. "I really didn't want to give him formula yet," she says. "I thought that was the surest way to get him to stop breastfeeding altogether."

By this time, the baby's pediatrician was getting worried. He still wasn't up to his birth weight, and as far as the doctor was concerned, the breastfeeding clock was quickly running out. Monika called her mother. She learned that there was a family history of low milk production.

"My mother said, 'Your grandmother had to supplement me,'" Monika explains. "She also told me that she had to supplement me and my siblings." Though Monika knew that many women of her mother's era were incorrectly told that they could not produce enough milk to feed their babies, her mother's story left Monika feeling strangely relieved. Maybe her problem really *was* genetic. Maybe she hadn't done anything wrong.

Breastfeeding experts now believe that inadequate milk supply is actually a relatively rare condition. In the past, the diagnosis served as a catch-all for women who actually were experiencing a host of common start-up problems like poor latch or sleepy baby. Formula was modern, easier, and more convenient, mothers were told. Why struggle to introduce a baby to the breast when something even better existed?

Today, well-intentioned lactation professionals insist that with a little help, most mothers can produce enough milk to feed their babies. Still, there are women like Monika who produce less than the optimal amount of breast milk. For those women, the feelings of frustration and guilt can be overwhelming.

"I was reading everything I could get my hands on, and every single thing I found said there is no such thing as low milk supply," Monika says. "One day, my lactation consultant finally told me, 'We think about eight to fifteen percent of women have a low milk supply.' Between gritted teeth I said, 'Don't you think it would be a good idea if you told women this?' We have all these depressed, anxious mothers crying into their nonalcoholic beer, and we're not telling them this? Isn't this the most patronizing attitude that women can't handle a minor degree of complexity? There's this attitude that if you tell them this is going to be tough, women are going to run scared and turn to formula. They encourage us to keep soldiering on in almost impossible circumstances. It's just like what they tell athletes: 'Play hurt.'"

Acting on the advice of her lactation consultant, Monika purchased a supplemental nursing system (SNS) and began feeding her son a combination of formula and breast milk. When she went back to work, her husband fed the baby formula from a bottle while she continued to pump at the office.

"The first time I broke down and gave him the supplement, he went right to sleep," Monika says. "At his first feeding, he sucked down an ounce or two. That was also the day he smiled for the first time. When he was finished eating, he looked up at me all content like, '*That's* what I'm talking about, Mom.' It gave me a feeling of relief *and* guilt."

Though she's still pumping regularly and taking herbal remedies, Monika has pretty much accepted the fact that her milk supply will always be lower than average. It's a hard reality to embrace, because for Monika, accepting a less-than-optimal milk supply means readjusting her self-image. She never thought of herself as a *formula-feeder*. Now she is, part-time at least. "When things were tough at the beginning, I thought, 'Some people have problems, but not me,'" Monika admits. "I have an earth-mother streak in me, and deep down inside I figured people like me always breastfeed without any problem."

As her son neared the six-month mark, Monika was still producing only enough breast milk for one or two feedings a day. "Eventually, I decided that maybe this is what there *is,*" she says. "I'm not going to quit trying, yet I've accepted that there may never be this magic moment where my milk starts flowing abundantly. I know he's a great baby and he's healthy and happy, but it sucks that this happened because I really wanted to do this for him and it hasn't worked the way I was hoping it would."

Welcome another unsuspecting woman to the wonderful world

of motherhood, where nothing works exactly the way you planned and a big, stinky load of guilt is always lurking just around the corner. When you've been saddled with as awesome a responsibility as the care and feeding of a child, it is only natural to feel like your parenting skills just don't measure up. But when a mama starts tearing herself apart for something she has no control over, starts feeling bad because she won't be in the running for Selfless Mother of the Year (the prize is a golden doormat, because that's what a truly *selfless mother* looks like), she needs to take a deep breath and realize that in the mamagame, perfection is unobtainable. It's our job to just do the best we can, and anyone who says your best isn't good enough—as California mama Kara put is so eloquently—can *go blow*.

Everything Monika read about breastfeeding made her feel like a failure, like she wasn't (despite the pumps and herbs and teas and tinctures) a good-enough mother. Because she had diagnosed herself as a breastfeeding "failure," Monika felt abandoned by all breastfeeders, as if other, more productive nursers were afraid of catching her disease.

"Partly because breastfeeding advocates have worked from a marginalized position for so long, their attitude has become kind of ideological and narrow," Monika says. "There is a frighteningly intolerant attitude out there about women who choose not to breastfeed. But there is also a real abandonment of women who have problems breastfeeding, because no one wants new mothers to think that these problems exist. I think the breastfeeding advocates make a huge mistake by not embracing the complexity of it, by not being honest about the experience. I think their insistence on a rose-colored view isn't doing any of us a favor. It sets up too many of us for failure if we define success so narrowly."

"I Just Can't Do It!"

Amy, a thirty-four-year-old communications director for a large Midwestern university, took it particularly hard when her attempts to breastfeed her infant son turned to near disaster.

From the outside, at least, Amy seemed to possess all the elements needed for a positive breastfeeding experience. She grew up with a mother who was an early nursing advocate, a committed member of her local La Leche League. Before her son was even born, Amy did her homework, reading up on breastfeeding techniques, purchasing a high-quality pump, and researching her employer's maternity leave policies.

In the years leading up to her son's birth, Amy had a hard time getting pregnant. Finally, she and her husband met with a fertility expert and were overjoyed when they were eventually able to conceive. But as it turned out, achieving pregnancy was only the first step on the long, tough road that lay ahead of them. For Amy, carrying a baby was anything but the glorious earth-mother experience she wished for. In fact, for nearly nine months she felt miserable.

"Nothing about my pregnancy was normal," Amy explains. "My breasts were huge and painful, I felt sick and tired most of the time, and I went into labor three and a half weeks early. I really didn't like being pregnant all that much."

Amy's son's birth was a surprise, but he was healthy enough to avoid a stay in the NICU. While a big, healthy baby is a good thing, big, bursting breasts are not. During her pregnancy, Amy's average-size breasts had grown to jaw-dropping proportions; in the hospital, they transformed into twin milk balloons, engorged beyond recognition and seemingly ready to pop.

"My breasts were so full that it literally looked like I had no nipples," Amy moans. "They were flat and stretched out. I just had these two huge, round balls where my breasts used to be. I showed them to the nurse and the lactation consultant that first day, and they both agreed that there was no way my son was going to be able to latch on."

To get her milk flowing—and her nipples in a latchable condition— Amy was advised to start pumping immediately. The idea was that a powerful hospital-grade pump might better stimulate milk production and pull her nipples from their now flattened-out condition. Soon,

Amy was able to produce enough colostrum—the early, antibody-rich substance produced by a breastfeeding mother—to feed to the baby in a bottle.

But despite her full-to-bursting breasts, Amy's milk didn't start flowing right away. Before discharging the anxious little family, the hospital's lactation consultant outfitted Amy with an SNS and advised her to continue pumping every two hours around the clock while feeding her baby formula at the breast. Amy also took fenugreek capsules—in the hope that the popular herbal supplement would help get her milk flowing.

After a week of painful, lumpy breasts, Amy's milk finally did come in "with a vengeance," she recalls. "I had milk everywhere. I was a sodden mess."

Being soaked with breast milk can be a pretty rotten (smelling and feeling) experience, but at this point, at least, Amy was the only one who seemed to mind. The baby, now off the supplement and getting all the fresh milk he could dream of, was content, fat, and happy. Amy's lactation consultant was excited that her advice was proving sound. And Amy's husband was happy to see their freezer fill up with expressed milk. Still, because she was now producing enough breast milk to feed a village of starving children, Amy decided on her own to tinker with her pumping schedule. Without consulting her lactation consultant, she began to abruptly drop pumping times in the hope that her body would stop producing so much milk.

It didn't take long for Amy to start feeling "icky," not sick enough to force a visit to the doctor, but enough to make her life feel pretty miserable. When Amy brought her son in for his one-month checkup, the pediatrician said, "The baby's fine, but *you* look terrible," Amy recalls. "Turns out I had mastitis and a staph infection."

Next, Amy went to visit the lactation consultant, who said that hers was the second-worst case of mastitis that she had ever seen. She also said that the infection had developed into an abscess, a dangerous, localized concentration of bacteria that, if ruptured, can be life-threatening. "They were talking about putting me in the hospital," Amy says. "The infection kept getting worse and worse. At one point, my whole shoulder was red, but I really didn't want to be hospitalized."

Amy was referred to an infectious disease expert. "As soon as he saw me, he said, 'This has got to come out now,'" she recalls. "Basically he gave me a local anesthetic and then he cut my breast open." As the doctor drained the abscess, Amy felt her dreams of breast-feeding her son start to drain away, too. "I just lay there on the table and sobbed and sobbed and sobbed," she says. She left the doctor's office with a breast wrapped in bandages and packed with gauze and orders to return to the office every day for the next month to have the wound cleaned and the gauze replaced.

Amy was at a crossroads. While only days before she had been determined to breastfeed, she was now so completely run down and exhausted that she lost all determination to continue. She wanted what was best for her baby, but she also had a reasonable fear for her own health. The emergency surgery freaked her out, and to be honest, the long recovery ahead made her feel like nursing would bring her more pain than pleasure.

"My breasts were never a big deal to me," Amy says. "I was al-ways the type of person who said, 'If I get breast cancer, lop 'em off.' But after going through this experience, suddenly my breasts took center stage. I felt so raw and physically spent. I was walking around with this big gaping wound. I couldn't look at my breast. It made me so sad and upset."

Amy's breastfeeding role model had been her mother, and now that she was considering giving up nursing for good, she felt like she needed her mom's permission.

"My mother loved to breastfeed," Amy says. "I knew that, and I wanted to be like her. Then, when things couldn't get any worse, she came to me and said, 'If you are doing this for me, don't. Take care of yourself. The baby will be fine.' That was all I needed to hear."

With that, Amy gave up on breastfeeding. She felt like it was the only thing she could do to preserve her sanity. She was tired of feeling sick, tired of feeling sad, and, truth be told, tired of thinking about her breasts all the damn time. But from an emotional standpoint at least, quitting was harder than she imagined.

"Even though I was pretty much constantly sick for the first eight weeks after my son was born, I still felt guilty the whole time, like I was hurting him, like I was a wimp for giving up, like I brought all this trouble on myself," she recalls. "Eventually I realized that I had to move on from this experience and start being a regular old mother. I couldn't do that when I was so focused on my breasts."

Amy's baby is now a toddler, and parenthood gets easier with each passing day. As the memories of those painful first few weeks fade, she's working on rescripting her vision of her son's early childhood, reminding herself that even though he had his share of formula (a product Amy still believes is "inferior" to mother's milk), he also had at least a month's worth of breast milk.

"The older my kid gets, the more I love being a parent," Amy says. "During so much of his early babyhood, I was sick. My husband was overwhelmed by being a dad for the first time. He was worried about me. We were at our wits' end for two months. Since then, he's been a super-easy baby, though for a long time the stress of those first eight weeks set a tone for his little life. We were constantly ready for the next crisis."

Corky Harvey, a lactation consultant and cofounder of The Pump Station, a superstore for breastfeeding mothers based in Santa Monica, California, says that many high-achieving mothers like Amy are blown away by the reality of breastfeeding when they realize that it isn't always easy or natural.

"I believe that breastfeeding has always been hard," Harvey says. "It's a learned technique. For most of us, it takes time and patience to get it right. We see a lot of accomplished professional women in our classes and at our store who are surprised by the fact that in most cases, breastfeeding just doesn't come naturally. They can write a business plan, they can get a client. But when these mothers encounter problems with breastfeeding, they can feel overwhelmed by what is essentially a natural function of their own bodies." And they feel frustrated that their bodies don't just "fall in line" and behave like the books say they should. Many, Harvey reports, express anger and frustration that nobody told them that breastfeeding could be tough.

Because Amy doesn't want other mothers to ride the same emotional roller coaster she did, she has decided to tell her story to any woman who will listen. It's not that she wants to scare mothers away from breastfeeding—she still thinks it's best for both mother and child—but she does want women to go into the experience with their eyes open. These days, Amy's creed is: *Information is more powerful than ignorance.*

"I've had women who have not yet had children tell me that I have been more honest—to a negative degree—about motherhood than any other woman they know," Amy sighs. "It's like we mothers are so busy protecting other women from the hard truths of this job that they go into it like I did, expecting that if you work hard enough at it, everything will be a breeze. When it isn't a breeze, they freak out. I had to go through all of this, to get torn down right down to my foundation, to come out stronger. If there's any way I can help other mothers avoid that shock, I will."

The Mama Advisory Board on Pain

- Michelle has no regrets about her surgery, but BFAR's **Diana West says she'd advise any woman considering breast reduction to wait until after she's had children.** "From my perspective, breast-feeding is such an important part of motherhood," West says. "Because reduction can limit your ability to produce milk, I'd wait to do the reduction until after you've had a chance to nurse your own babies."

- **Try rethinking your definition of "success."** Experts agree that any amount of breast milk is better than none. At first, Monika, who needed to supplement because of low milk supply, thought of herself as a failure: "But then I decided that I'm doing the best I can, that my son won't suffer just because he's having some formula. When I did that, I stopped thinking of myself as a bad mother."

- "If you have a child with special needs, **seek out all the support you can,**" advises Julie, whose son was born with a cleft lip and palate. "Once you get to know other people who've been through the same thing you're going through, you begin to realize that it doesn't have to be the end of the world. It helps you feel stronger."

- Amy suggests that you **listen to as many breastfeeding stories as you can**—good ones, bad ones, *and* ugly ones: "Ask people to tell you what it was like for them. You've got to go into it with your eyes open. You've got to understand that for most of us, there's more to it than just sticking the baby on. If you hear the stories ahead of time, if you ask questions, you'll be more prepared, and things will probably go easier."

Chapter 8

Romancing the Pump

Suddenly, it's Take-Your-Breasts-Back-to-Work Day

A federal investigator, Mary led a glamorous life. As a member of the government's elite army of private eyes, she'd travel around the country in search of fraud, interviewing illusive suspects and uncovering costly scams. Before she went out on assignment, Mary made a point of preparing for anything, loading her car with the tools of her trade—maps, notebooks, badge. Then her son was born, and Mary began to throw one more piece of essential equipment into her trunk: her breast pump.

A working mom hauling a fancy briefcase-cum-breast-pump rarely raises an eyebrow in the corporate world these days, but in the male-dominated field of federal investigation, Mary was an anomaly. The job requires employees to spend much of their time on the road, and "mothers' rooms" for lactating employees are about as rare as PETA members at a pig roast. But Mary was committed to breastfeeding her son, and because she had to return to work when he was still very young, she devised a plan for pumping on the go.

"When I was working in the office, I'd take regular breaks, but when I was out on the road doing interviews, I pumped in a lot of parking lots," Mary confesses, laughing. "I got really good at it. It's easier than you think to pump discreetly while sitting in a car. First thing, I bought one of those hands-free attachment kits. That way I could still get work done while I was pumping. I also got a battery pack so I could run my pump anywhere. Then I'd pull into a parking lot, put the pump in the passenger seat with a jacket over it, and prop some work up on the wheel of the car. I don't think anybody ever noticed what I was doing."

Mary's son is her first child, and so, like most greenhorns, she thought that she had the whole work-family thing figured out well before his birth. Because her employer offered only six weeks of paid maternity leave, Mary decided to come back to work right on schedule. Her husband would stay at home with their son during the week and work three weekends a month. And when Mary needed to travel for her job, the whole family could go along. Sounds simple, right?

"I was in a fog, thinking that it would all be peachy," Mary says, reviewing her carefully designed pre-baby plans. "But after my son was born, it quickly became clear that things weren't going to work out the way we expected them to."

I think there's a breed of hardworking mamas-to-be out there who believe flexibility is something that's best limited to yoga class. I know about this phenomenon firsthand, because I was that kind of woman—and I think Mary was, too. Like Mary, I figured that if I planned everything out ahead of time, returning to work after baby would be a breeze. I cut back my schedule, toured day care centers, and bought a cute little pump and a supply of nursing-friendly bottles. But then I gave birth to an adorable little being who weighed little more than a Cornish game hen and whose helpless cries had the power to turn me to Jell-O. It didn't take long for me to realize that for the next few months at least, there was a new boss in town. Mary was about to learn the same lesson.

First off, Mary and her husband had to search high and low until they found a bottle that the baby wouldn't just spit out of his mouth.

And even after they found one that he would accept, the baby mostly just snacked from the bottle when his mother was away, preferring to get his milk straight from the source. Then, as the couple adjusted to their newborn's erratic sleeping schedule, they realized that traveling with an infant who fussed several times a night might be harder than they thought. As the days quickly turned into weeks, Mary watched as her maternity leave slipped through her fingers. She didn't want to go back to work—but she felt like she had to.

"I suffered from this horrible guilt," Mary says now. "As the time to go back approached, I was starting to panic. But I couldn't think of any other way to do it. I felt so bad for my son, and I felt so bad for me. I felt inadequate, like I was a bad mother, abandoning my child when he was just six weeks old."

Maybe it was guilt that motivated Mary to stick with nursing, even when the demands of her job made it tough. Because she wanted to keep her milk supply up once she went back to work, she needed to pump at least three times a day—in the women's bathroom, in her car, and even in an unlocked resource library at her office. ("I'd put my back to the door and cross my fingers," she recalls.)

For the first couple of months, Mary's boss was "pretty accommodating," she says, but it didn't take long for her to get the message that he was becoming frustrated by the amount of time that the pump was taking out of her day. It was a vicious cycle: As her boss began to take note of the frequency and the length of her breaks, Mary started to suffer from what could only be called performance anxiety. Soon it began to take longer and longer to pump even the smallest amount of milk from her breasts. (And it's not like Mary *enjoyed* her time with the pump. Any woman who's ever used one on a regular basis will tell you that they are a necessary-but-miserable invention. Though they remain bulky, noisy, and uncomfortable, pumps have come a long way from their predecessors, but regular use can still make a mother look and feel like a dried-out dairy cow.)

"It was taking me a long time to pump," Mary explains. "I was sitting there for as long as twenty minutes during my morning and afternoon breaks." And because he didn't much care for the bottle, Mary's son developed a pattern of what experts call reverse-cycle nursing, taking in very little breast milk during the day and stocking up during the night when his mother was close at hand. This meant that he was waking up every two hours all through the night to nurse.

Even though Mary and her husband were co-sleeping with their son, this new feeding schedule was frustrating, because the entire family felt exhausted by morning. And Mary's boss had stepped up his not-so-subtle antinursing campaign.

"Once, he informed me that he had 'told' his wife to quit nursing when their child went into day care at five months," Mary says. "By the time I went past the five-month mark, I knew that his patience was wearing thin." Something had to change.

Though she really liked her job, Mary started checking out other employment options, and in a couple of months she found work as a fraud investigator at a statewide WIC office. It would be pretty ironic if a federal agency known as the Special Supplemental Nutrition Program for Women, Infants, and Children had a poor policy on pumping. It didn't take long for Mary to discover that supervisors at her new office went out of their way to make life as easy as possible for lactating mothers.

"This place has a mothers' room that has a hospital-grade pump," Mary explains. "You can use the office pump or you can use your own. Everybody's incredibly supportive. They allow you as many breaks as you need to pump. When I travel to other offices, there are usually mothers' rooms and pump rooms there. If there aren't, someone is always willing to give up their office. The work environment here is very supportive from the top down." And because her new employer offers flextime options, Mary now works five nine-hour days and takes every other Monday off to be at home with her son.

"I'm just really happy with my new situation," Mary says. "I loved my old job in many ways, but this position gives me the flexibility to be more of the kind of mother that I want to be. It has made our lives so much easier."

Reality Check

I'm happy that things worked out for Mary, but let's be realistic here: Most working mothers don't have jobs that are nearly as accommodating. While nine states (California, Connecticut, Hawaii, Illinois, Minnesota, New York, Tennessee, Texas, and Washington) have passed legislation requiring—or at least encouraging—employers to provide "reasonable accommodations" for breast-pumping mothers, according to California attorney and breastfeeding advocate Alexis Martin Neely, all legislation is not created equal. "The last time I checked, there were seven states with strong laws and two others that encouraged companies to make accommodations for breastfeeding mothers but did not require it," she says. "That's not what I'd call a clear mandate."

Even if you lump all states with workplace breastfeeding legislation together, that still leaves forty-one states that don't provide any legal support for a mother's right to take comfortable, uninterrupted pumping breaks at work. That means that if you choose to breast-feed your child *and* go back to your job, odds are you'll be pumping at the whim of your employer. And if you work at a job where it's hard to take regular breaks (food service, manufacturing, or law enforcement, to name a few), you may have to make a choice between breastfeeding your baby and making a living. For many women in today's economy, not making a living just isn't an option.

Despite what many politicians would like us to believe, this isn't the 1950s, when most mothers stayed home to care for their children, and many middle-class families (back then, "family" meant a married heterosexual couple and their 2.5 offspring) got by on the income of a single wage-earner. A number of forces, including economic need and personal choice, have converged to mean that more and more American women with young children are now working outside of the home than ever before. According to the U.S. Department of Labor Statistics, more than half of American mothers of children younger than one year old are now employed, many on a full-time basis. Our economy now depends on the contributions of all workers regardless of gender to keep things going full-steam ahead.

This reality presents a number of challenges for modern working mothers, who, like Mary, have to grapple with guilt, face down bull-headed bosses, and perform daily sleight of hand just to squeeze in a few minutes alone with a pump. The daily juggle can make a mama feel more like a broken-down milk machine than a source of life and maternal sustenance, and make breastfeeding for more than a few weeks feel next to impossible.

Not so many years ago, formula seemed like it could be a way to welcome more women into the workplace. But as more and more research pointed to the advantages of breast milk and the official line became "breast is best," things got complicated once again. Now, for many women, the choice to breastfeed a baby breaks down along economic lines. If you are lucky enough to have a job that offers adequate maternity leave and accommodations for pumping (usually a white-collar job with good pay and benefits), your child can be breastfed. If you have a job that provides no paid maternity leave and no pumping accommodations (usually a nonunionized blue-collar or service-industry job), your child will likely be formulafed.

Sociologist Linda Blum, PhD, believes that the economic system as it exists in America today provides very little support for nursing mothers, be they white- or blue-collar. Even if a woman is fortunate enough to have the economic support she needs to stay home and care for a child full-time, breastfeeding requires a high level of commitment. To work and breastfeed requires a combination of dedication and luck that many women simply do not possess. What's needed to raise breastfeeding rates in this country, Dr. Blum argues, is not lip service to the now-accepted notion that "breast is best." Rather, we need a nationwide commitment to recognizing and supporting the economic needs of *all* mothers, an idea that sounds too radically socialist for our current political climate. Dr. Blum writes in *At the Breast:*

> "Many in the medical community express concern that the modern workplace is hardly 'baby friendly.' However, they use their authority to recommend little in the way of workplace or public-policy reforms. Instead, the medical profession solves the wage-earning/breastfeeding dilemma by glibly advising mothers to use breast pumps. An employed mother, in other words, can feed her baby at the breast at home, but she should collect her milk and keep up her supply by using a pump (or expressing milk by hand) during work time. In fact, the AAP's [American Academy of Pediatrics] recent statement prioritizing longer breastfeeding mentions only the need for employers to provide space and time for breast-pumping. The AAP fails to mention options that would allow mothers more time with their infants, such as increasing the Family Medical Leave Act, which now provides just twelve weeks of unpaid leave."

Because she's her family's top wage earner, Mary doesn't think giving up her job is a viable option—though there have been many times when she's considered it. While her new workplace makes being a parent that much easier, she still wishes that there was another option, a way for her to take time off to care for her son while still making ends meet for her family.

"There are some things that I would miss about work," Mary says. "I would miss the intellectual challenge of it. I wonder if I were home full-time if I would be crawling the walls by now and yearning for adult conversation and something interesting to work on that involves a higher level of my brain. I think if somehow, magically, I had the opportunity to stay home, I would find ways to keep myself interested and my son happy. Even when I'm with my son for long stretches, even when things get challenging, I never find myself wanting to get away and *work.*"

The Land of the Not-So-Free

It just doesn't make sense. Or, sadly, maybe it does. As Americans, we live in what has been called the richest nation on Earth, yet we work harder and longer than almost anyone else. While other countries require employers to provide as many as six weeks of paid vacation a year, the average American gets only two, or ten paid vacation days. The news isn't any better when it comes to maternity leave. Parents in Sweden—the country with the world's most generous parental-leave policy—are eligible for ninety-six weeks' leave at 80 percent salary following the birth of a child. Other countries with generous maternity policies include Norway, Denmark, Australia, and Canada.

One could argue that it's not all that surprising that industrialized Western nations with strong histories of public policy can choose to provide such benefits to their workers. But how do you explain the fact that poorer, developing nations (take Ethiopia, which offers mothers ninety days paid leave at 100 percent salary) provide better maternity benefits to their citizens than the United States, with its paltry mandated twelve weeks unpaid leave for companies employing more than fifty people? Worldwide, only a few countries—Singapore and Swaziland among them—provide weaker maternity leave provisions for their citizens.

"As a nation, we tell our citizens that work is much more highly valued than personal life," Dr. Blum says. Sending such a message would be simple enough if our country's leaders were also declaring, "Formula is just as good as breast milk," but they are not. Instead, we increasingly get the message (from government health agencies and respected mainstream organizations like the AAP) that "good" mothers breastfeed their children for at least a year. But because successful breastfeeding often requires time, support, and commitment, and because employers aren't required to give workers the paid time off needed to succeed at this goal, many mothers end up falling short. Work and motherhood begin to look like siblings vying for their mother's attention.

"We've been taught to think about women advancing career-wise in a way that makes family-friendly ideas like attachment parenting and extended breastfeeding and child-led weaning pretty impossible," Dr. Blum says. "It's hard to see how the demands of a full-time job can make that other reality even remotely possible."

Like many well-meaning working mothers before her, Shannon, a thirty-six-year-old vocational rehabilitation counselor and mother of one from Los Angeles, sketched out her One-Year Plan well before her daughter was born. She would take a four-month maternity leave—enough to really get to know her baby and make sure that breastfeeding was established—and then continue nursing for at least one year. While she was away at work, Shannon would pump and store breast milk.

It was a great plan, a workable scenario that countless mothers have managed to pull off effortlessly. Or so it seemed to Shannon—until she got back to work and realized that being a mother isn't always as effortless at it seems. Her daughter's birth and early nursing were challenging, but the pair managed to get the hang of things by the time Shannon had to return to work full-time. Once she was back at the office, Shannon quickly realized that it was harder than she thought it would be to make time for regular pumping breaks.

"I was keeping a very busy schedule at work, and so I'd only be able to break away to pump maybe once during the day," Shannon says. "That left me with going five or six hours without pumping. After about two months back at work, my milk supply started to decrease, and my daughter needed to have formula during the day while I was gone. Eventually she became much less interested in nursing. For a time, I tried to pump more often, but I wasn't as aggressive about it as I should have been," she sighs. "Things got beyond my control without my really even noticing it. If I had the chance to do it again, I would definitely pump more often at work."

By the time Shannon's daughter was seven months old, she had made the switch to 100 percent formula. Things had gotten particularly consuming at work, Shannon explains, and one day she realized that she had gone more than twelve hours without pumping. She worked late, and when she got home, she tried to get her little girl to nurse, but the baby had a different idea. "She just turned away," Shannon says. "She completely rejected me. I felt horrible, so, so guilty."

Shannon admits that her daughter's rejection of the breast wasn't the only thing making her feel guilty. The truth was that while she loved the sensation of nursing, she wasn't particularly fond of all the behind-the-scenes work needed to keep her supply up while she was away from her daughter all day. She knows that she probably could have made pumping work if she'd been more diligent about it, but she enjoys her demanding job. When she's needed at work, she prides herself on being there. Besides, she's not sure how her supervisors would take it if she had to step away from the action for twenty minutes or more three times a day.

"I tell myself that it was good that she got breast milk for six or seven months," Shannon says. "Everyone says to me, 'It's okay, don't feel bad,' but I still do. My mom kept saying, 'Babies don't nurse forever, Shannon.' I'd respond, 'But I wanted to do this at least for a year.' I feel ashamed that I gave up so easily. I guess it comes down to the fact that I just wasn't able to do my job *and* breastfeed at the same time."

Making Breastfeeding at Work *Work*

Let's switch to a "glass-half-full" perspective for a moment here. For every working mother like Shannon who finds the demands of breastfeeding and full-time work incompatible, there are many who manage to continue nursing—despite a demanding job. Sometimes, it just takes time, determination, and a clear sense of your rights.

Kristin, the 32-year-old account manager, lives in Minnesota—one of the states that Neely identifies as having the most progressive breastfeeding and work laws—so when she returned to her job after her three-month maternity leave, she felt it was within her rights to ask her employer to set aside a clean and comfortable place for her to pump.

"When I first got back, there was no designated lactation room at work," Kristin says. "So I went to my office manager and complained. I was angry because at that point my only option was to pump in the restroom. It was the only private place. I told myself, 'I'm going to change this. It isn't right.'"

Kristin encountered a number of roadblocks on her quest for a clean, well-lit pumping room, but because she knew she was committed to breastfeeding for the long haul, she kept at it, pestering one supervisor after another and slowly making her way up the corporate food chain.

"The office manager told me she couldn't help me," Kristin recalls. "So I talked to human resources. Then I was referred to the head of human resources, then to our national human resources representative, and finally to one of our vice presidents. To each one I said, 'This has gotta change. We are a company that has 75 percent female employees. Of that 75 percent, 80 percent are in their childbearing years. If you are going to have a workplace that looks like this, you have to offer these kinds of benefits.' It worked."

To say Kristin's campaign worked is an understatement. Her employer now has at least one lactation room in every one of its offices around the nation. Each lactation room has a door that locks, a comfortable chair, a refrigerator, and a hospital-grade pump. "When you have a baby, you can bring your own pump to work, or you can just order the attachment kits for the office pump," Kristin says, a little proudly. "The company even gives each new mother a little refrigerated bag stocked with a freezer pack and bottles."

Kristin has been in the corporate world long enough to know that she wasn't single-handedly responsible for her company's progressive breastfeeding policies. But she knows that sometimes the sound of a few wheels squeaking together can make a significant change.

Kristin travels quite a bit for work, and when she was breastfeeding, she always made a point of making sure that her needs would be accommodated. At first, she was afraid that such requests would throw clients for a loop, but she soon learned that if she adopted a matter-of-fact, "it's for my baby" attitude when making her requests, most people wouldn't complain.

"Before I went to meetings out of the office, I would tell my contacts, 'I am breastfeeding and I am going to need to break from our meeting at this point to pump. Do you have a private room where I can do that?'" Kristin recalls. "My customers were all very understanding. No one batted an eye."

But not every workplace is as understanding. This is America, after all, and ordinary people still get the giggles when the subject of breasts comes up. Add to that the idea of a coworker using a machine to pump and store the fluid that comes *out* of her breasts, and you're likely to encounter a few awkward silences—or even a silly joke or two. Back when I was pumping regularly, I worked in an office full of sweet, progressive-minded folk, but that didn't stop one of my coworkers (his office just happened to be right outside the moldy, abandoned shower room I had convinced them to let me pump in) from saying, half joking, "You can do this—but *please* don't let me hear it."

"Even in the better jobs where you might have the autonomy to use a breast pump in the privacy of a pumping room, the whole idea of pumping is still seen as somehow unseemly," Dr. Blum says. "Many women don't want anyone to know what they are doing when they go on pumping breaks. They try to slip away unnoticed. You don't want people thinking of you that way. And then there are the jokes that go around offices about someone accidentally picking up—and drinking—a bottle of their coworker's breast milk. We still don't know how to handle this in a natural way."

When it came to finding a place to set up her pump, Siri, curator at a large modern art museum, took a more indirect approach than Kristin did. "I work with several people who I knew would not be tolerant of the idea of me getting in their faces about breastfeeding," she says. "So I never came out and said, 'I have to pump.' When I needed to, I'd just sort of slip silently away. I never mentioned breastfeeding at all. I just took it upon myself to find a private place where I could pump."

And unlike a corporate office, an art museum presents few options for private pumping. "We have this modern, white, minimalist interior," Siri says. "When I first got back from maternity leave, I did a search of all the bathrooms, looking for a place to pump. I had to look at the bathrooms because there was really no other place for me to do it. It turns out that in the whole building, there was only one private bathroom with both a lock and an outlet. There was nowhere to sit, though, just a little sink and a toilet. So I had to take one of the folding stools that our tour guides use and carry it with me every time I needed to pump. The bathroom was on the sixth floor, so I'd take the pump and the stool up there two times a day. Every time I'd be pumping away, I'd always wonder if people outside could hear the little motor going 'wrr-wrr.' I'd be sitting there the whole time on this little stool, leaning over my pump. It was uncomfortable, to say the least."

Pumping can be a logistical nightmare, even for an exceptionally organized mother who's committed to long-term breastfeeding. "Nursing is nice," laughs Linda, a forty-seven-year-old college professor from Athens, Georgia. "But pumping stinks. There's no other way to put it. The whole working-mommy juggle is very hard when a baby is small. I just remember the blur of exhaustion. I had to make these extensive lists just to get out the door in the morning. I don't know how I did it."

Rachel, a former history professor and current nonprofit director, was breastfeeding her nine-month-old when she got a job interview at a college in Ohio.

"Academic job interviews last for at least a full day," Rachel explains. "Usually they are more like two days, and they keep you busy the whole time, giving talks and going to lunch and dinner and meeting with other faculty members."

Rachel wasn't ready to wean her daughter, so she made a point of telling the person who called to set up the interview that she was breastfeeding and that she would need a private room where she could pump. She packed a small manual pump and crossed her fingers.

"When I got there for the interview, the woman I had talked to on the phone showed me around for a while and then handed me off to another woman," Rachel recalls. "She told the other woman that I needed a private place to pump, and she said, 'I know just the place for you.' Instead of a private office like I'd imagined, she took me to a women's bathroom on campus that had a public lounge area right by the door. I felt pretty uncomfortable about this arrangement, but by that time I *really* needed to pump. I tried telling the woman, 'I'll meet you downstairs,' but she said, 'That's okay. I'll just wait here with you.' This was one of the people who was going to be interviewing me later. It dawned on me that I was going to have to sit there and pump right there in front of her, then later tell her why she should hire me for a job. I couldn't imagine a more awkward situation."

Rachel tried turning her back and pumping. "I was still so uncomfortable that I don't even know if I got any milk out at all. We both tried to make conversation, but it was just so awkward. I've always been fine with nursing in public, but I wouldn't pump even in front of my own husband." Sadly, after all that, she didn't get the job.

Sometimes, even when the odds seem like they are stacked against a mother's long-term breastfeeding success, she manages to keep going, pumping milk for her child and succeeding at work. Doctoral student Deborah Dee had to go back to work only seven weeks after her daughter was born. She was determined to make breastfeeding work despite her busy schedule. "It was of the utmost importance to me that my daughter never have formula," she explains. From the start, Dee set out to get as comfortable as possible with her pump—and to get her daughter as comfortable as possible with the bottle.

"First off, I tried to never look at pumping as a *duty*," she says. "I will admit that pumping is not the same as nursing. It is not as easy or as enjoyable. Basically, it's kind of a pain. But I was determined to do it. I didn't care what it took. There were even times when my nipples were cracked and bleeding, but I didn't care. I kept pumping. I knew that if I was going to do this for an extended period of time, I needed to toughen my body up. I was determined to breastfeed my daughter, and I did it. Sometimes I wonder, if I had had the slightest ambivalence about this decision, would I have given up? To my advantage, I have financial resources and a supportive husband and a fairly flexible job. Not every working mother can say that."

Dee also wants to make it clear that in the end, the time she spent with her pump never felt like a sacrifice. More accurately, it felt like a luxury.

"It's such a privilege to be able to breastfeed," Dee says. "I did it myself, and because of me, my daughter thrives. Tell me: How lucky is that?"

The Mama Advisory Board on Nursing While You Work

- **Before you go on maternity leave, talk to your boss about your plans to breastfeed,** Kristin suggests. But even before that, do your research. Some states have legislation that encourages (or even requires) employers to provide pumping facilities for workers. "Find out in advance if they will be providing you with a comfortable place to pump and time to do it. If they don't, try to convince them that they should."

- **Get comfortable with the pump before you go back to work.** Deborah Dee suggests starting a regular pumping schedule while you're still on maternity leave. "That way, you can be confident about using the pump once you're at work. And you'll even have some milk saved up ahead of time."

- **If you have to travel for work, call ahead to let them know that you will need a place to pump,** Rachel says. And just in case the facilities aren't up to par, remember to pack a battery pack—or at least a manual pump. "It might not be perfect, but it sure beats not being able to pump at all."

Chapter 9

The Party's Over

To wean or not to wean?
That is the question

This could either feel like a beacon of light on the horizon or a sad reality of life: At some point, every mother stops breastfeeding. Some start thinking about stopping not long after they've begun. Others find that nursing becomes such an important and rewarding part of their lives that they feel like they could go on forever. Usually a mother (or, regrettably, another outside adult force) leads the charge to stop nursing, but sometimes it's the kid who makes the final decision to quit.

No matter how it comes about, no matter if it feels traumatic or natural for the parties involved, the truth is this: Weaning happens.

Anthropologist Katherine Dettwyler, PhD, famously studied the average weaning ages of primates, humans' closest ancestors. She concluded that if left to their own devices, human children would likely wean at or around the same ages as apes, orangutans, and gorillas—somewhere between two and a half and seven years. Even though she knows that Western social mores don't allow for many seven-year-old nurslings, Dr. Dettwyler still advocates for the nutritional, emotional, and developmental benefits of extended breastfeeding, a stance that has elevated her to hero status in the attachment parenting world.

"You have to consider the needs of the individual mother and look at the individual baby," Dr. Dettwyler says. "That said, weaning at six months is not biologically normal. When babies come out of the birth canal, they don't know they are Americans," she says. "They don't know that our culture expects them to stop breastfeeding at a specific time. All they know is that they are little baby primates. Their bodies are going to expect to nurse for two and a half to seven years, and to them *that* is normal."

What seems normal for one baby might feel abnormal to another. Timea Szalay is a lactation educator and mother of four from Innisfil, Ontario. While she knows that many children continue to nurse happily well into their preschool years, she's come to the conclusion that most kiddies decide to call it quits long before they're old enough to ride two-wheelers.

"This isn't the case for every child," Szalay says, "but I generally find that babies wean themselves sometime between 18 months and three years."

When Szalay started having children, she decided that she was going to let her babies determine the way they wanted to be breastfed. "From the start, I knew that I was going to let my children lead the way," she says. "I was going to let them decide on their own when they wanted to nurse, how much they wanted to nurse, and to have their own way of weaning themselves." Her first children, a set of twins, abruptly stopped nursing at four-and-a-half months. Her third child stopped taking breastmilk when he was less than nine months old. Both weanings took Szalay by surprise.

"My twins just quit one day, and there was nothing I could do to get them to start again," she recalls. "I was terribly sad about it, but I was also so overwhelmed by being a new mother that I didn't know what else to do. My third stopped taking the breast when I had pneumonia and I had a high fever. I was very sick and on antibiotics. I don't know if that's why he stopped nursing, but for some reason he just stopped one day. I often think I could've stopped taking the antibiotics, that maybe that would've brought him back, but eventually I told myself he stopped when he wanted to."

When Szalay gave birth to her fourth child, she took the same child-led approach to breastfeeding as she had with the other three. This time things are different. Her youngest son, now three-and-a-half, is still nursing about three times a day and once at night. Both mama and son are happy with the arrangement.

"Because the twins quitting so young was a disappointment, when my third went to five months I said, 'Wow. This is all bonus,'" Szalay says. "I viewed every extra day as a benefit for me and my child. Now, with this son I continue to say every day is a bonus. I'm very happy with the decision I've made to keep nursing him as long as he wants. Maybe it's partly because he's my last child and it's a way of me hanging on to this part of my life, but when he wants to quit, I'll support his decision."

Before I became a mother, I had no idea that weaning could be a controversial topic, touchy enough that many breastfeeding guides offer only the slimmest advice on how to make it safely through this big transition. (A few books do offer good weaning advice, though, and board-certified lactation consultants can also a great source of information.)

In the not-so-distant past, many doctors and mainstream parenting gurus argued that after the first year or so, breastmilk provided little nutritional benefit for children. In recent years, however, most medical experts have changed their tune, and new research has discovered that breast milk continues to boost the immune systems of kids well into the second year of life, maybe even further.

That's great news, but plenty of mamas who've nursed their babies past the traditional definition of "babyhood" have gotten their share of grief from friends and family who encourage them to stop nursing the minute the sight of a growing (or talking or walking) child at its mother's breast starts to make them feel uneasy.

Szalay tells her clients to ignore the critics and keep on nursing for as long as they—and their babies—want. "Breastmilk is the best food for babies," she says. "No matter if you nurse for just a week or for years, breastfeeding provides emotional benefit as well as protection and immunity for your child. No matter what the age of your child, your breastmilk is made specifically for him. Every day your child gets milk from your breast is an amazing bonus for both of you."

Blessing or Booby Trap?

Dimity, a thirty-two-year-old writer from Santa Fe, weaned her daughter at eight and a half months. Breastfeeding came easy to her, and for the most part she enjoyed it. Still, when the time came, she was more than ready to quit.

"I really wanted my body back," she says. "I was sick of my daughter getting to dictate what I was going to do. I was sick of not being able to run comfortably and be an athlete. That's an important part of who I am. Having a child was such a big lifestyle change anyway. I wanted at least one part of my life to feel more normal."

Dimity weaned her daughter over a series of weeks by gradually introducing formula, cutting out one breast-milk feeding at a time until she was just nursing her baby before bed at night. After that, it was just a matter of gradually cutting back on the nighttime feedings. "There were a couple of nights when I got pretty uncomfortable," she recalls. "I'd have to get up and get in the shower and express some of the milk out."

While Dimity felt perfectly satisfied with the amount of time she devoted to breastfeeding her daughter, she was also aware that eight months of breast milk didn't quite meet community standards in her über-crunchy hometown.

"Here in Santa Fe, we are La Leche League poster children," she says. "If you don't nurse for at least a year, people act like it's not worth anything." But when Dimity, who had moved to Santa Fe from New York, would call her friends back on the East Coast, the reaction was markedly different: "They'd be like, 'Oh my God. You're *still* nursing?'"

Dimity doesn't remember the last time her daughter nursed. The whole experience seemed to wrap itself up naturally, with her daughter eating more and more solid food and slowly turning more toddler than baby. Now that she's done it once, Dimity says that she could imagine nursing a second child for longer than her first, but she hasn't made any promises to herself—or anyone else. In the end, nursing was a good experience for everyone involved, but looking back on it doesn't make Dimity misty-eyed with longing.

"I appreciated the time we spent together," she says. "But it wasn't like the magic moments you see in Hallmark commercials. A lot of time I'd be reading a magazine and watching TV. I wasn't just gazing down at her lovingly."

Tasha, a thirty-four-year-old professor from State College, Pennsylvania, often wonders how she could give birth to two children with such markedly different attitudes about nursing. Her oldest daughter was a marathoner: She nursed avidly and devotedly until well past her fifth birthday. Tasha's youngest was more of a sprinter: After a strong start, she resolutely weaned herself before she was nine months old.

It's not like Tasha *planned* to nurse her first child until she was just months away from starting kindergarten. It just happened.

"I didn't think about breastfeeding much until I was pregnant for the first time," Tasha explains. "But after she was born, breastfeeding turned out to be so easy and enjoyable. At first, I planned that I'd nurse her for a year. Then, during that first year, they came out with the information that a year was good but two years were even better, and so I thought, 'Okay. Two years max.' But then two years turned to three, and three to four. Before I knew it, I was pregnant with my second and still nursing my first."

When Tasha's younger daughter was born, tandem nursing worked well enough—at least at the beginning. Because the big girl nursed just in the morning and evening, this would give the baby plenty of uninterrupted time at the breast, Tasha thought. Her eldest, on the other hand, sometimes saw her little sister as an interloper.

"When the baby was born, my older girl did get a little bit put off, because I insisted that the baby get to nurse first so she'd get the best milk," Tasha recalls, laughing. "I would make her wait until the baby was done nursing before she could take a turn. Sometimes she'd whine and complain about it, and I would say, 'You're lucky to be nursing at all, kid.' Then she'd get with the program."

When Tasha had her first child, she was still in graduate school, and her more flexible student schedule made it easier for her to make time for breastfeeding. Though her daughter went to the campus day care during the day, the center was in the same building as Tasha's office, and she'd run down there several times a day to feed her. By the time her second was born, Tasha had found work as a professor, and the demands of the job meant that finding time to break away for nursing was much harder.

"I just couldn't make it down to the center as often as I could the first time around," Tasha says. "When my youngest was about six months old, I asked the people at the center, 'Why don't you guys give her formula during the day?' They were fine with that, and surprisingly I didn't feel guilty at all."

Tasha now partially blames the introduction of formula for what happened next. "The baby had been having formula at school for a couple of months when she just stopped nursing one day," she recalls. "She was eight and a half months old. One morning I got ready to nurse and she just refused. I kept trying for a few days, but she kept refusing. She just stopped cold turkey. She'd turn her head away like she knew what she wanted." With a resigned laugh, Tasha admits that she was more than willing not to force the issue. "At that point I'd been nursing kids for a long time, and so I was kind of ready to stop."

The baby may have been finished with nursing, but Tasha's preschooler was still going strong. They went on this way for several months—the baby drinking from a bottle while the big girl continued at the breast. Even though she knew in her heart that there was nothing wrong with nursing an older child, Tasha soon began to daydream about weaning her big girl once and for all.

"I started to feel like, 'This is getting weird,'" she explains. "Eventually I told her that she was getting really old, and it was time for her to stop nursing. 'You are going to start kindergarten in the fall,' I explained. 'You've gotta stop by the time you're in school.'"

At first, Tasha's daughter actively resisted her mother's plans, but Tasha remained firm: "When I'd tell her that we were done with nursing, she'd grumble and get upset," she says. "At some point, when she wanted to nurse before bed, and I'd said, 'No,' for the thousandth time, she asked, 'How about if I just *pretend* to nurse?' That was fine with me. We snuggled up and she pretended to nurse. She still does that to this day."

Maybe because her daughters' nursing histories were so different, Tasha says she pays special attention to the differences in each child's personality. Some differences aren't all that surprising. "When my oldest was a little kid and she'd be playing with her dolls, she'd lift up her shirt and pretend to nurse them," Tasha says. "My little one doesn't do that. She feeds them a bottle." But some are more subtle. "The baby is more outgoing," Tasha says. "The oldest is more inward." Though she has some regrets about the way she handled this key part of her youngest daughter's babyhood, Tasha also believes that the experience helped give her a more realistic idea of the struggles most nursing mothers go through.

"I'm not an activist," Tasha says, "but I do think that because of my experiences I'm now pretty sympathetic to women who don't want to nurse for very long. Before my youngest was born, I might not have felt that way. The funny thing is that sometimes I feel like I have a closer relationship with my little one—even though I bottle-fed her."

Grand Finale

Whether they nurse for five months or five years, most mothers will tell you that weaning is a bittersweet experience.

A mama who has been dreaming about trading in her saggy old nursing bra for a racy, lacy new underwire will still likely be moved to tears when the last feeding finally arrives. I felt that way: torn between my dual desires for freedom *and* a continuing deep connection with my child. Freedom eventually won out, but I can't deny that I still sometimes feel guilty for making what many might see as a selfish—rather than selfless—choice when it came to my child. Innocently (or was it ignorantly?) banking on the future, I told myself that if I ever had another child, I would do a better job at this key element of mothering.

In the end, I breastfed my oldest daughter for just over six months. That's longer than most mothers in the United States (in 2003, for instance, the Ross Mothers Survey found that only thirty-three percent of nursing mothers were still going strong at the half-year mark). But according to the American Academy of Pediatrics, six months is not long enough. They recommend that at a minimum, mothers breastfeed their infants for twelve months. The World Health Organization goes even further, recommending breast milk for two years.

If I gave in to my guilt over this topic, I could easily spend the next forty pages detailing the reasons why I stopped nursing. But I'm resisting the urge, understanding full well that my decision was mine, that any dime-store psychologist has already figured out my reason for writing this book in the first place. Suffice it to say that by the time I wrapped things up with Baby Number One, I was sick of being sick. (Remember my run-ins with Mr. Mastitis?) I was tired of pumping, tired of feeling overwhelmed, overworked, and underappreciated. To this day, though, I still feel bad about weaning her when I did.

I don't remember our final nursing session. Rather, I remember a series of quiet endings, a gradual tapering to a point when our nighttime cuddlings no longer included milk from my breasts. Because I knew the end was near, I cried a little during those final feedings, remembering both the wonderful moments and the frustrating ones. But I wouldn't be honest if I didn't admit that I also felt lighter, freer when it was all done. As we were tapering off, I asked my sweet baby to understand that I needed to separate from her in order to become a better mother. My daughter smiled sleepily and rubbed my earlobe with her soft fingers. I told myself she was giving me her blessing.

Kristin, the thirty-two-year-old account manager who "joyfully" breastfed her son until he quit at seventeen months, still remembers the last time he nursed. "Somehow, somewhere in my heart I knew that this was going to be the last time he nursed," Kristin recalls, the memory making her eyes mist. "It was the day he turned seventeen months old. I was nursing him to sleep like I usually did. It was spring, and I had the window open so I could see the stars, and he was cuddled up next to me. It was a very emotional moment for me. It was hard to give it up because I knew I wasn't going to have that closeness with him anymore, but for weeks he had been giving all the signs of quitting, and I wasn't going to force him to do something he didn't want to do. Breastfeeding to me was so intimate, and that's one of the things I loved about it. It really was one of the most beautiful things that I have ever done in my entire life. I couldn't help but feel sad because that chapter in our lives together had come to a close, but I also felt deeply, truly blessed to have been a part of it."

The Mama Advisory Board on Weaning

- One mama, Sandy, a thirty-five-year-old nonprofit administrator from Seattle, **took a trip each time she weaned her daughters.** "Both times, I was getting down to just one feeding a day," she says. "I went away and left the baby with my husband." From Sandy's perspective, this was a healthy way to make a clean break from nursing her toddlers. "I was ready to end it, and this way they had their father there to distract them. Plus, I got a vacation out of it."

- When you're approaching the time to finally call it quits, re-member how **Tasha cut a deal with her oldest child.** "I told her that we could still cuddle at night, but we weren't going to nurse anymore. It was hard on her at first, but eventually she figured out a way to make it work for her. She asked if she could pretend to nurse, and I said okay. So we still have the closeness, but I also have my body back."

- Nursing an older child? **If someone comments on your nursling's "advanced age," be prepared to respond with a snappy come-back,** suggests lactation educator and nursing mother Timea Szalay. "If some day I'm out breastfeeding my toddler in public and someone asks me, 'When are you going to stop nursing him?' I'm going to say, 'In the next five or ten minutes,'" she laughs. "I've never had any negative feedback yet, but preparing myself, just in case, has always made me feel more confident."

Potato Pulp, Nursing Tanks, The Buddy System: What I Learned the Second Time Around

As soon as my first child was born, I started giving everything away.

Convinced that one baby was *enough,* I pressed piles of barely worn onesies and rompers on every new parent I knew. As our daughter grew from infant to toddler, I gave away the pump, the swing, the bouncy seat—all the cumbersome detritus of modern parenthood.

It's not that I regretted having Baby Number One—not one bit. My husband and I were hopelessly, shamelessly in love with our little Bug, but *I,* at least, was so freaked out by the awesome responsibility of caring for her that I couldn't imagine ever doing it again—especially now that the reality of the job had been revealed to me.

Back then, if someone had asked me to write down the things that made first-time motherhood tough, it wouldn't actually have been a very long list. Sure, there was labor, but in some freaky way I actually *enjoyed* giving birth. Then there was sleep deprivation, which was tougher (and longer-lasting) than labor, but even that eased up eventually. Also on the list would be unexplained night-time crying jags, diaper rash, illnesses, and all the sorry—but still expected—stresses of babyhood.

But breastfeeding—the thing that invariably topped my list—was not something I expected to stress about. Not at all.

Yet I did, and maybe somehow all the clumsiness, infection, tears, and guilt that this so-called natural act inspired in me turned breastfeeding into a metaphor for my ability (or inability, rather) to be a good mother. Months later, while part of me was sad to be done nursing my baby girl, another, bigger part was relieved, ready to wash my hands, put that "failure" behind me, and get on with raising my wonderful (and I thought *only*) child in the best way I knew how.

Then, slowly, predictably, something changed. As my daughter grew, as my love for her threatened to burst out of my swelling heart, I began to forget most of what was so hard about her first few months in the world. As she turned one, and then two and then three, I began to think that maybe having another baby wouldn't be so bad after all, that most kids eventually *do* sleep eight—and even twelve—hours in a row, that diapers eventually give way to underpants, that sickness seems less traumatic in a sturdy four-year-old than in a fragile infant. Call me crazy, but I began to want another baby.

I've heard it said that the techniques used in brainwashing (sleep deprivation, isolation, blind obedience to a tyrannical leader) are similar to the experiences of new parents, and so it may be that our brains were thoroughly washed. Somehow, my rosy-hued memories of pre-baby life, with its luxurious, uninterrupted nights of sleep; unencumbered sex life; and freedom of body, mind, and spirit began to fade. I began to see the forest rather than the trees, to realize that those mind-numbing first few months of parenthood were just *months,* after all, with years of something much better still to come.

Once Bug Number Two was firmly planted, I set about thinking of ways I could make the experience of early infanthood easier—for Baby *and* for me. Some of it came down to nurturing my hard-won sense of perspective, to realizing, in a nutshell, that *this, too, shall pass.* But I also realized that if I was truly going to use experience to my advantage in dealing with tantrums, teething, and toilet mastery, I'd also have to take a close look at what made breastfeeding so tough for me the first time out. I wanted to believe that somewhere deep inside of me (and inside every other mother, too) lived a sassy, sexy nursing pro. All I had to do was roust her out.

Here We Go Again

For once, my timing was perfect (though unintentional), and my second pregnancy progressed along with the writing of this book. As I interviewed one amazing breastfeeding mother after another, I was taking my own private crash course in nursing, assembling an all-star Mama Advisory Board. More than once I found myself thinking, "Why didn't I know this last time?"

It's not like every pregnant woman gets to (or would want to, for that matter) spend nine months reading, writing, and talking about breastfeeding. But as it turned out, that's more or less what I did. As this second baby grew inside me, so did my determination to give breastfeeding another try, to do everything I could to make this experience a little easier than it had been the first time. Like it or not, the internal pressure was building for me to get breastfeeding "right" this time. I *was* writing a book on the subject, wasn't I?

I've always been perfectly comfortable seeking professional help, so when I was faced with the prospect of yet another hungry little mouth to feed, I did some research and found myself a lactation consultant who was willing to provide a little prenatal "lactation counseling." I wasn't looking for *therapy* in the traditional sense of the word. What I wanted was someone who could talk me through some everyday strategies for avoiding the common nursing mishaps that had tripped me up the first time, namely a poor latch, overabundant supply, and one too many encounters with mastitis. I placed a phone call, explained what I was looking for, and scheduled an appointment for about a month before the baby's due date.

When the day of our meeting finally arrived, Lynn, the lactation consultant, showed up armed with a handwritten list of preventive measures designed to help me avoid mastitis. We'd deal with the latch and supply problems when—and if—they ever happened, Lynn told me confidently. (Confidence! Optimism! I liked her already.) As far as avoiding Mr. Mastitis (and his gentler cousin, Ms. Plugged Ducts), there were a few things I could do ahead of time to limit the chance of a reoccurrence, Lynn assured me.

First, she suggested two supplements—at least 1,000 milligrams a day of vitamin C and 400 milligrams of lecithin with each meal. Both were time-proven ways to help prevent a mother's milk from backing up and getting infected, Lynn explained. Then, with a subtly raised eyebrow, she passed over The List.

Because I've never taken kindly to lifestyle restrictions, Lynn's suggestions looked (to me at least) like something you'd see on a cell-block wall:

- Loose clothing, especially bra. No underwires.
- Don't carry shoulder bags. Use hands.
- Rotate sleep positions—back is ideal.
- Avoid saturated fats in diet to decrease plugged milk ducts.
- Once periods come back, limit salt intake several days before each period starts.
- Wear cabbage leaves in bra—known to be anti-inflammatory.
- Place potato pulp on affected area three to four times a day until symptoms subside.

If I've learned anything in my months of research and writing, I've come to understand that for most mamas, making breastfeeding work is *work*. In order to do it right, you have to put your money where your mouth is—metaphorically at least. And because I really wanted breastfeeding to be more enjoyable this time around, I swallowed my pride and told myself that shoulder bags will *always* be in fashion, that underwires are uncomfortable anyway, that sleep deprivation makes any sleeping position feel luxurious, and that saturated fats and salt aren't all they're cracked up to be. Cabbage leaves and potato pulp were another thing altogether. I told myself I'd save them for moments of true desperation.

Then it was just a matter of weeks before my second baby came hurtling into the world. When she did, I again felt unspeakably honored to give birth to her, to finally touch the warm, slippery body that I had felt squirming inside of me for all of those months, to at last breathe in her sweet, musky baby scent.

When the midwife placed this second beautiful infant on my chest, I was immediately transported back four years to another delivery room in the same hospital. So many things were the same—the same wise midwife, the same steadfast, loving husband, the same sounds and smells—but somehow *I* felt remarkably different. As I brought this new baby to my breast, I realized that this time I was armed with the knowledge and experience of the women I'd spent the last six months talking to. I felt a surge of confidence, like I had a gaggle of gals, a militia of mamas standing at my back. Right then and there, I knew that everything was going to be okay, that this time things were going to be easier.

And they were—more or less. Amazingly, after a few false starts (including my second night in the hospital, where I broke down and gave in to the newborn nurse's offer to give my baby a few ounces of formula—just so we both could sleep for a couple of hours), this kidlet and I have become one of those shameless, infection-free, breast-milk-only mama-baby nursing teams, the kind I grudgingly envied back when Baby Number One and I were still struggling along. At this writing we're still going strong, with no wean date in sight.

Though the list of people who've never been lucky enough (ha!) to see this nursing mama in action is still pretty long, I've become so confident of my ability to breastfeed discreetly that I *have* whipped 'em out in some pretty public places. (When I do nurse out in the open, I'm often reminded of a pal of mine who once told me, proudly, "A lot of people have seen me breastfeed, but I don't think a stranger has ever seen my nipples.")

When I think about how self-conscious public lactation used to make me feel, I recall with pride the recent sunny autumn afternoon where, in an effort to calm my fussy six-month-old, I lifted my

T-shirt and cracked open my nursing tank right there on the sidelines of my older daughter's soccer game. No one blinked an eye. (What I've realized since is that no one ever does.) When I finished with this particular feeding, the mother who had been sitting next to me the whole time noticed that I was burping the baby. She said, admiringly, "Did you just nurse her? I didn't notice." Insignificant as it was, this felt like a small victory.

The fact that nursing has gone so much easier this time around feels like a blessing from the Big Mama In The Sky, a consolation prize to make up for all the heartache my boobies dished out five years ago. But this newfound realization that breastfeeding, the thing I had once assumed would be the easiest, most natural thing in the world, actually *could* be the easiest, most natural thing in the world has opened my eyes and made me a kinder, gentler, less judgmental woman.

Because the first time around I was one of those mothers who broke down and quit breastfeeding before my baby reached the magic age set by the experts, because, in my earlier incarnation, I was one of those "evil, selfish" working women who felt (for lack of a better phrase) *sucked dry* by nursing and pumping, I understand all too well why some new mamas decide to throw in the towel. But this time, because things have gone better all around, because my work life has changed to more easily accommodate breastfeeding, because I've gained some kick-ass supermama role models, I've developed a new appreciation for the hard work of mothers who choose to stay home full-time to care for their children. I'll say it again: Nothing is easy. No choice is perfect. But for me at this particular point in time, and for this particular baby, things seem to be working out just fine.

Now that you've heard this particular ending to this particular breastfeeding saga, please don't imagine my story fading to black with a montage of soft-focus mother-and-child shots and a sappy easy-listening soundtrack. It wouldn't be my life—or yours, let's be honest—if everything wrapped up so gracefully.

Imagine, instead, a mostly happy mama doing the best she can, a hardworking woman with plenty of embarrassing, awkward, graceless moments, but also enough beauty and wonder and joy to keep her going for the rest of her life. That's me. And that's enough. While I'm smart—and cynical—enough to realize that things could fall apart any day, for now my cubby little nursling and I are happy. So are her big sister and her father. And that's more than I could've ever asked for, more than I ever dared dream of.

Thirsty for More?

Recommended Breastfeeding Advice, Information, and Resources

Awesome Breastfeeding How-To Books

Nursing Mother, Working Mother: The Essential Guide for Breast-feeding and Staying Close to Your Baby After You Return to Work, **by Gayle Prior**

Whether they have to or they want to, some mothers return to work while their babies are still breastfeeding. Unlike some more strident tomes, this book accepts that fact—and provides helpful advice and timely solutions for combining nursing and work. I wish I would have known about it after my first daughter was born.

The Nursing Mother's Companion, **by Kathleen Huggins, RN, MS**

I was given this book during an early appointment with my midwife. While the photos and line drawings of happy/hippie parents (dads with Grizzly Adams-style beards, moms with granny blouses and long, middle-parted hair) have turned off many a modern-day mama (myself included), the knowledge-able how-to-nurse advice in this book helped me through many a rough patch. There's a reason why this book is in its fourth printing: It's a classic guide that no nursing mother should be without. (I also want to give Huggins props for writing *The*

Nursing Mother's Guide to Weaning, a topic that many breast-feeding experts like to ignore.)

The Nursing Mother's Problem Solver, by Claire Martin

While this volume's reference-book format can feel a bit awkward (do I look up Plugged Ducts under *P* or *D*?), it adopts a lighthearted—at times even humorous—tone that so many other breastfeeding guides lack. A good addition to your booby bookshelf.

The Ultimate Breastfeeding Book of Answers, by Jack Newman, MD and Teresa Pittman

I'll admit that I was put off by the idea of a male breastfeeding expert, but this Canadian physician is a true milk god, a kindly and committed wise man full of sound advice on just about anything to do with nursing, from proper latch technique and combining breast milk and solids, to the safety of medications during lactation. Many lactation consultants swear by Dr. Jack's advice, and now I know why.

Your Baby and Child, by Penelope Leach

This wonderfully illustrated (four-color photos of cute British babies!) parenting book provides clear-headed, gentle advice on early breastfeeding. Maybe it's because she's a level-headed English lass, but Leach's even, nonjudgmental approach to childrearing is different from many popular Stateside guides. Parents either appreciate Leach's mellow tone or get annoyed that she doesn't come right out and state her opinion. Personally, I like that she lays out the choices and leaves the final decisions to her readers.

While We're on the Topic of Breasts

The Breast Book: An Intimate and Curious History, by Maura Spiegel and Lithe Sebesta

Speaking of breast obsession, this clever little gift book is an illustrated history of the female breast. Give it to your favorite nursing mama, or throw it into your diaper bag and read it flamboyantly during your next public nursing session.

Fresh Milk: The Secret Life of Breasts, **by Fiona Giles**
This book's News-of-the-Weird mix of booby-based memoirs, musings, and maunderings is a great read during those post-partum days when your breasts are just about all you can think about. Australian author Giles's look at modern attitudes about breastfeeding is witty, insightful, sexy—and even occasionally disturbing.

www.glamourmom.com
I can't say enough about these gorgeous cotton/Lycra nursing tanks! These are a dream come true (for the moderate-to-modestly endowed mama, at least). I wear them all the time. And when I'm finally done nursing, I'm afraid it will be hard to give them up.

www.lalecheleague.org
You gotta give the brave women at La Leche League credit for all the hard work they've done advocating for breastfeeding mothers and their babies. This massive site is full of general breastfeeding news and information, as well as contacts for LLL groups in your hometown and around the world. If you ever have a nursing emergency, you can also find a real, live nursing mother who can help talk you down from the ledge. Talk about amazing.

www.pumpstation.com
Even if you don't live in California, you can still pay a visit to The Pump Station, the first breastfeeding superstore. But it's not just commerce: This Web site provides sound information about nursing, as well as an easy online way to purchase bras, clothing, and equipment. While you're there, check out the funky latch-on video.

General Mama/Baby Support

Baby Love: A Tradition of Calm Parenting, **by Maud Bryt**
Somehow I picked up a copy of this book when I was pregnant with my first child. I'm so glad I did, because this gentle, no-nonsense parenting guide made caring for a newborn seem

easy. The beautiful black-and-white baby photos also helped me get excited about the little bean that was scheduled to arrive.

The Big Rumpus: A Mother's Tales from the Trenches, by Ayun Halliday

In her trademark edgy, honest style, Halliday reveals the strange realities of raising two young children in the middle of the big city. Read the book and then subscribe to Halliday's über-cool 'zine *East Village Inky.*

Brain, Child: The Magazine for Thinking Mothers (www.brainchildmag.com)

There aren't any other parenting magazines that come close to this amazing quarterly, jam-packed with essays, editorials, and features on modern mothering. A must-have for any sassy mama.

Operating Instructions, by Anne Lamott

Lamott's beloved parenting memoir tells the sometimes-painful truth about a woman's rocky first days as a mother. Once you read Lamott's desperate recounting of her son's first few weeks, your own life will seem much easier.

Index

Underscored page references indicate boxed text.